Jungle Freeze-Frame

Barry Seymour Brett

This is the Rainforest - these are the people You'll laugh & you'll cry as you enter their world and share their way of life

These thought-provoking humorous stories feature life in the Jungle City of Iquitos and the surrounding Rainforest, highlighting our weaknesses and their strengths.

Each article is a portrayal of actual events as seen through the eyes of a Californian living in Iquitos, Peru.

SOUTH AMERICAN STANDARD EDITION

This South American Standard Edition contains 155 pages and more than 70 black & white illustrations of the people and places featured in the stories.

JUNGLE FREEZE-FRAME
South American Standard Edition
First Published MARCH 2010
ISBN: 978-0-615-35628-0
Text Copyright; Barry Seymour Brett

A collection of short humorous stories written during 2009 & 2010 and assembled in book-form with various copyright dates as indicated beneath each individual article.

Special thanks;
to Aldelberto Antonio Cordova for permitting the use of the photo of his son, together with several monkey photos which were better than mine!

to Captain Bill Grimes at Dawn on the Amazon Tours and Mike Collis, editor of The Iquitos Times for their encouragement.

DISCLAIMORS

Save the Eco-Coffee
The person handing-out Adopt-a-Thon leaflets was not an employee of Starbucks' Coffee! Starbucks does help many small impoverished communities in Africa and South America.

Fantasy Trap *is a FANTASY and any resemblance to reality is solely in the eyes of the beholder. Like most Americans I am a regular customer of Walmarts and I admire their efficiency and pricing.*

At a Fund-Raiser for Street Orphans, Iquitos, Peru.

Intro by the Author

In all of my articles I try to portray actual events in a humorous way. The reader will be tempted to believe that all the situations described are pure fantasy and bare no relation to reality. Nothing could be further from the truth. Veronica the Pirate, Wilber the Tarot Card Man and Victor the Midnight Planter are all real people. Cheverengue, Michael (La Gallina) and Oscar (Mala Suerte) all live in the neighborhood and can often be seen walking along the Amazon Boulevard. They, together with many more characters that appear in my stories, represent the pageantry that is "The Amazon Jungle".

A few names have been changed to protect the privacy of individuals. I was present at all of the events described and experienced all of the situations mentioned in my work.

The majority of these stories were written for English language newspapers and magazines here in South America. Others were written for internet sites catering to tourists.

In many of my stories I contrast the culture of the Amazonian Jungle Peoples with the cold, calculated indifference of the Californian Lifestyle. Anyone planning or dreaming about visiting the Rainforest will find my articles to be of great value in learning the "Inside Story".

Barry Seymour Brett

The Location

Almost all the stories feature events in or around the Amazon river-communities and the rainforest. Most of the articles revolve around the City of Iquitos, smack in the center of the Rainforest. Isolated and with no roads connecting the city to other parts of the nation, Iquitos nevertheless is a vibrant and colorful community. With almost half a million people, it is by-far the largest city in the world without connecting roads. With only a small airport, almost all trade and commerce moves by river transport.

As you read my stories it will become abundantly clear that Iquitos suffers from extreme poverty. Amazingly, the inhabitants are literate and for the most part, unlike other South American Cities, enjoy a relatively tranquil crime-free life. The language is Spanish although the village tribes and their relatives living in Iquitos speak Quechua. The modern version of the ancient Inca language, Quechua nevertheless has been superseded by Spanish, the language of commerce, radio and television. Attempts to revive Quechua have not been successful.

Iquitos currently has widespread internet access together with cell phone service and cable television. Few people can afford those luxuries. Outside of the city the overwhelming majority live from day-to-day without electricity or running water.

INDEX TO THE STORIES

Beauty in Death

THE PASSING OF A BABY GIRL

Barry Seymour Brett

It was a beautiful Iquitos morning. After a jungle breakfast I took a quiet stroll toward the Belen Market. I was looking forward to drinking a "Jugo", a blended fruit drink. All kinds of jungle fruits with strange sounding names are blended into exotic tasting drinks. I passed-by the street stands selling sunglasses, wallets and cell-phone cases. I looked for my young friend Lewes. A street vendor, 23 years old. I had known him since he was 18. Lewes had worked for me on and off but in his heart he was a street vendor. An older man approached me with the sad sorry news. Lewes was at home with his three week-old baby girl. Sadly she had passed-away at the local hospital the night before. He thrust a paper in front of me, listing contributions and donors' names. Glancing down the list of donations I realized there was no way Lewes could afford the expense of a funeral. I raced to the house on the outer limits of town.

On the way over I cast my mind-back to my own impending doom some five years earlier. Undergoing chemotherapy for a cancer at stage four, I had the unpleasant experience of visiting a funeral home to check on prices! There she stood. The Saleswomen. Dressed in black pants, white shirt and black tie. As she stared at me with that cold deadpan face I felt I was already dead! Then the thunderbolt came-down from the sky. "It's for you isn't it!" "Why, Yes but - Yes it's for me, but how did you know? Do I really look that sick? "We always know Mr. Brett - **we always know**!" she said as she reached for the measuring tape. "You don't expect to be around to see it Mr. Brett. That's why you chose the cheapest one!" Suddenly I had visions of the handles falling-off or the bottom falling-out before I got to the cemetery. I rushed-back inside to order a more expensive but more durable model! She noticed my bald head. "Would I be needing a hairpiece?" Then there was the question concerning the cemetery plot. Did I want it encased in concrete to prevent the earth from crushing-in, disfiguring my good looks? If I splashed-out for the earthquake resistant model she would throw-in the hairpiece at no additional cost!

Finally I arrived at Lewes's house. He lived in a small community half a mile or so from the main road. The mototaxi driver, fearing he might get bogged-down in the mud, refused to take me to the house. Trundling down the pathway to the house I passed another motokaro struggling to get out of a mud-hole. Neighbors rushed to his aid. Up to their wastes in mud they tugged and pulled until finally the mototaxi was dragged-out of the quagmire onto solid ground. That's Odd. I don't remember neighbors, or anyone else for that matter, rushing to my aid when I broke-down in heavy traffic in Downtown Los Angeles. People stood around and stared. Drivers passing-by, passed-by! Not even a friendly face. I was afraid to abandon my car lest they stole my tires!

As I approached Lewes's house I saw a group of people assembled outside. The small casket stood inside but in full view of people passing-buy. All the neighbors in that impoverished village had come-together for him. Luis, an orphan, had no family to help-out. Those beautiful loving, caring, poverty-stricken people had raised the money for the casket and were only short the money to hire a bus for the burial service the following day. Children were out combing the neighborhood for suitable flowers to make wreaths and bouquets. Village families showed-up with their children and grandchildren to view the casket and the little girl within. An older woman lit some candles and as I hugged Lewes we stood before the little girl and prayed. It was tragic, yet peaceful and serene. On my way-back to the main road I could see other villagers carrying flowers with their children, wandering down the muddy pathway to pay tribute to the little girl whose life had so tragically been cut-short. Some of them had walked for two or three hours!

The following day, sitting in a mototaxi on the way to the cemetery I contrasted the difference between the loving caring lives of the jungle people of Iquitos and the Amazon and our own cold Californian indifference to everything including death. "Oh Honey, there's been a death in the family." "Not now Dear, I'm watching the game". "Can't it wait 'till later!" "Just send an email and shop-on-line for some flowers and that earthquake resistant model. That should take care of it. Wamart's had it on sale last week!" "Oh, and remind them to put the funeral on U-tube!" "I might want to check-it-out!"

As I waited outside Punchana Cemetery for the bus to arrive, I couldn't help noticing the sharp hairpin bend in the road immediately in front of the entrance. Motorbikes, cars and yes, buses swerved across the median into opposing traffic. There were many near misses. How convenient. Good for business I thought! And so close! Just a hop skip and a jump! Two hours later, and still no bus, (What was that about being late for your own funeral)?

I was getting thirsty waiting around in the midday sun. I walked up the street looking for a soda-stand. Suddenly there was a loud thunderous roar as a bus turned the corner almost running me down as it sped to its date with destiny. Tipping to the side as it swerved into the hairpin bend the bus screeched to a halt in front of the cemetery gates. Overloaded and crammed with adults and children in every corner and others hanging onto the back and sides. I wondered where the casket was, or even if they would be able to find it amongst the abundance of humanity!

These wonderful villagers assembled together in front of the cemetery gates and wandered-up the pathway holding bouquets of flowers and carrying the casket before-them. There was an air of sadness and yet relief that this little child would finally rest in peace. Yes there were tears, including mine, but somehow it was refreshing. All these villagers coming together in time of grief to pay their final respects to a child they could scarcely have known. A brief service was held, the casket lowered and then the most wonderful moment came. All the children, I counted more than thirty under ten years old, picked the petals-off the bouquets and placed them lovingly on her grave. An amazingly colorful display of jungle flowers and fauna. As we walked-back down the pathway I decided that when my time comes I would like to rest in peace at Punchana Cemetery. I would be honored to be buried next to these people, even without a hairpiece. I wondered who might attend my burial service and shower my grave with jungle flowers. At least two people would be there. Me and the guy with the shovel!

Caravana

Barry Seymour Brett

Supporters of CNI join the Caravana

The clock struck midday, and already they were sitting outside my door waiting to go to the game. With six entradas (tickets) to Max Austin Stadium in my back-pocket my friends were assured entry. Soccer is the life-blood of Iquitos. You'd better watch-out for your life, and there will be blood! But wait a minute, who's he? I didn't invite him! "Where's Carlos?" "Carlos isn't coming, he's an Allianzista!" "Oh really, from which planet, Mars or Venus?" "No Barry, Carlos supports Allianza Lima. He only goes to Allianza games" "Allianza Lima! But Lima's over a thousand miles away, why would he support Allianza?" "Because they win Barry. They win!!!"

Feeling somewhat despondent I hailed two motokaros to take us to the Stadium. Outside the Stadium, waving the college flag, wearing their quernos and conos (team hats), their faces painted in the colors, my friends shouted the familiar chant of their team - CNI. The College Team of an isolated Peruvian City, situated on the banks of the Amazon and surrounded by thousands of miles of rainforest, had suddenly found its' day in the Sun. Ridiculed, derided and languishing at the bottom of the league for oh so-many years, suddenly (miraculously) CNI found itself within a hair-breadth of the ultimate prize, the CUP! Outside the stadium, seats near the supporters of the opposing team (the expected winners) were selling at three times the price of seats for CNI. Illegal bookies, working out of a local bar ran odds heavily against CNI! My friends rushed to place their bets.

It was rowdy. There were screams of anger and joy. Police in "full-metal-jacket" raced up and down the aisles quelling one outbreak after another. Spectators, their jungle blood screaming for vengeance and a win, became more and more agitated. Vendors standing in the aisles were pushed and shoved, their cakes and popcorn trampled-upon, as people squeezed-by to get a better view. Waving their banners and pounding on their jungle drums there were constant threats and shouts of foul-play. Things were reaching fever-pitch. The ground vibrated and the stands shook as fans jumped up and down in their seats, shaking their fists in a show of solidarity. Then the referee blew the whistle. KICK-OFF. The game commenced!

Leaving the stadium after the game there was a sense of disbelief. Supporters poured into the street, over-whelming the vendors selling hamburgers and sodas. How could it have happened? What did we do to deserve this fate? All those long years in the wilderness of the rainforest have finally come-down to this. Underdogs forever and a day and now, and now - "WE'VE WON!" Yes we've won. The CUP is ours. The table's turned and now we're the winners!

The following day we assembled with thousands of supporters in Plaza 28th July to view the "CUP" and listen to speeches from the soccer-players and the City Mayor. Lewis and Gabriel suggested we should hire a motokaro so we could participate in the "Grand Caravana". A procession of several hundred motokaros would wind its way around the streets of Iquitos waving flags and banners. Caravanas were not uncommon, but this would be bigger and better than most. Leaving plaza 28, we gained speed rapidly, accelerating at red lights and crossing the median strip into opposing traffic. Police stood-by but did nothing. Pedestrians that dared step into the roadway, quickly jumped-back onto the sidewalks as the Caravana sped-on proclaiming its victory throughout the villages and city districts. Hollywood Freeway on a Friday afternoon, I thought. Without the graffiti, guns and sign language!

Daniel, Jay and Lewis displaying the College Flag outside Max Austin Stadium, Iquitos, Peru

Daniel and Gabriel waiting for the kick-off

There were nasty incidents when overloaded motokaros carrying nine or ten supporters, overheated and broke-down or tipped-over, delaying the procession. Passengers fell-off, sustaining minor injuries, only to rejoin the parade by clinging to the sides of subsequent motokaros. Whole families rented motokaros to participate in this victory parade. Mum, Dad, six or seven kids and Grandma and Pops. They waved flags, chanted the slogans and drank what appeared to be coca-cola! It smelt a little different. Something like that unauthorized chemistry experiment at school, oh so very long ago. You know the experiment I mean. The one with the "Still!"

The Caravana winding it's way through the streets of Iquitos

A young CNI Supporter

The Prize on display in the Plaza 28.

Villagers in the suburbs lined the sidewalk to view the procession and show solidarity with their victorious home-team. Spectators and passers-by climbed trees and street poles just to get a better view as the Caravana raced past with a tremendous roar. Suddenly we took a sharp bend and tipping toward the side hit a pothole in the road. It was the end of our day on the Caravana. We sat at the side of the road as streams of motokaros continued their daring drive into the sunset. I thought about all the tickets California Highway Patrol (CHP) could have written this day. They would need to cut-down the entire rainforest just to supply the paper!

Friends passing-by picked-us-up and drove us home. There was just the question concerning the damaged motokaro. Who would pick-up the tab? I turned to my friends. "Well Guys, you made-out like bandits with those bets you placed." "I think it's time you anteed-up." "But Barry, uh, well we didn't, we didn't mean to." "But, well, we bet against CNI. We just didn't think they could win!" I slumped-down into my armchair in total disbelief. How could they? What kind of team-players were they? These lifetime jungle supporters wearing team colors, chanting the chants, waving the College Flag, their bodies engraved with CNI tattoos. I didn't have the heart to tell them, but whatever happened to team pride and loyalty? After my friends left I was faced with the thorny issue of the motokaro repairs. There was just one problem - I couldn't pay either. I also bet against CNI!!!

Twilight Zone at the Penal

Barry Seymour Brett

Lunch-Break in the Guard Tower!

My friend's neighbor, Robinson was in trouble. Visiting him at the jail, I handed the guard my ID. "Robinson muerto (dead), he muttered. Oh, this is terrible, so sad I thought. I'd spoken to his mother in the morning. She urged me to go visit him. Handing me a bag of food and toiletries, she gave me directions to the "Penal". I guess she thought he was still alive; after all you can't feed a corpse! How did it happen? Why are they letting me in? I guess they want me to view the body and pay my last respects.

Inside the entrance were numerous inmates selling their handicrafts and souvenirs. Who I thought would want a souvenir of his days in the "Penal"? Beautiful wood-carvings of boats and tropical birds, paintings of prison life, furniture and household items were on display. Missing was a set of keys! As the guard led me through the jail I heard someone call-out. "Barry!" It was Robinson! There he was up-front, alive and in person! "But Robinson, the guard told me you were dead!" "No Barry, didn't you know that all my life people call me "Robinson Muerto". I'm so thin and sickly-looking. Even Mom and Dad call me "Muerto" he said, as I handed him the bag of food, toilet paper and soap.

Waiting for passengers!

First stop was the church followed by the canteen. Inmates were sitting at tables in a large hall. There he was, "Cheverenge", smiling and walking toward our table. "Cheverenge", that villain of the Amazon Boulevard. The cigarette vendor who seemed to be selling everything except cigarettes. The guy who sold my stolen camera back-to-me! Surrounded by four thugs, one of them sat down opposite me, his muscled-up body rippling as he leaned-over to welcome me and crush my hand. "They call me "Hulk". Why, I wondered. "The Hulk" was a wimp compared to this guy. I felt intimidated. "Don't worry Barry he's gentle as a mouse." "He's here to protect you". Gentle as a mouse? It's funny but somehow I felt safer before they arrived. I decided to cover all bets and buy them a meal. Yes, "buy!" There were windows with bars and a slot to slide the food (and the money) through. Inmates with access to money ruled the "Penal." Without money you were hostage to hunger. Cheverengue showed me his new jail tattoo. Spread halfway across his chest, there it was, in full color. "The Nike Logo". Trademark infringement I thought. He could go to jail for that! They gulped down the food like there was no tomorrow, and in this jail there might not be! "Hulk" looked at me with those "gentle as a mouse eyes". Oliver Twist, I thought. (Please Sir, can I have some more? - or else!). Without hesitation I rushed-over to the window to order a second plate, and a third if he wished!

They took me on a four-star tour. The "Penal" was like a small town with numerous streets. Those with money lived on a special section, the Beverly Hills of the "Penal". Somehow they had electricity, Big Screen TV's, running-water and their own restaurant and general store at the end of the street. Some inmates had been there twenty years! But wait a minute. Where were the bright orange jumpsuits, the black and white striped pajamas with ball and chain? Inmates wore their own clothes! Prison garb was not supplied. In this jail you wear what you arrived in.

There were other visitors with their relatives and kids. Everyone arrived with food for their loved ones. Low quality food was provided for inmates free of charge. But like those "Burger King Two-for-One Coupons", only when available and on "a limited basis!" What kind of food was on the menu I wondered - when available? Cheverengue filled-me-in. "Caballo y Burro con arroz." (Horsemeat & donkey with steamed rice!). Visitors wandered up & down the streets and in & out of the cells! What they really needed was a "Michelin Guide of the Penal", listing the best accommodations, canteens, tattoo parlors, churches, carpentry shops and discotheques. Yes, there was even a "discotheque! Men, whose wives or girl friends came on a visit, could "arrange" with the guards for a vacant room. "Outside catering!" was available for an additional fee. If they couldn't afford an "arrangement", inmates (Hulk & his buddies) would kick people out of their cell, install a stereo system complete with disco-ball and stand guard in-front. "Hulk" leaned-over toward me. "There are girls available right now" he said as he winked at me with those "gentle as a mouse" eyes.

Walking toward the "better-section of town" I noticed the ominous guard tower ahead. There was an inmate up-top. But wait a minute, an "inmate!" Yes, it was definitely an inmate. How could that be? I turned to Cheverengue. "Look, there's a prisoner in the guard tower!" "No Barry, he's a guard." "A Guard!" But where was his uniform? He looked like all the other inmates. Wife-beater shirt and a baseball cap! Cheverengue smiled. "Guards have to supply their own uniforms, it's wash-day or he can't afford one!" "But how can they tell their own guards from the other inmates?" I asked. Cheverengue laughed out loud. "It really makes no difference Barry. Guards have to supply their own ammo. That's why they don't have any!"

It felt like the "Twilight Zone". Guards without ammo or uniforms! Discotheques and "Outside Catering!" Where I wondered was "Death Row" or the "Chain Gang!" cracking rocks. Everyone seemed to be having a good time! Cheverengue pointed-out that the punishment was not being able to live with your family and friends. Oh really! Would that include my mother-in-law?

It was getting late. 'Hulk" felt thirsty. Instantly I sat myself down at a table to order-up some sodas. "Coca-cola, Hulk?" "No, I like "Pilsen!" "But "Pilsen", that's beer. "Yes, that's what I like, beer." There it was, chalked-up on a board. "Beer, 15 Soles a bottle (five times the street price). Airport prices in a jail? "O.K. "Hulk", but no more that two". For a short time we sat around drinking and talking. Inmates (underdogs) from other impoverished streets dared not enter our "Avenue of the Rich and Infamous." They stood at the far end looking enviously down the street as "Hulk" downed a couple of beers. Finally it came time to leave. What an interesting day-out I thought as we struggled to carry "Hulk" back to his cell!

Copyright August 2009

IQUITOS WATER CARNIVAL

Barry Seymour Brett

The Humisha Tree blossoming with Gifts

It all started so innocently. A casual knock at the door. "Would you like to contribute to the "Street Humisha Fund?" "Well, uh maybe. Just a moment". I rushed over to my Spanish-English dictionary. No mention of it there! "I'll get-back to you later". My mind raced-back to the contribution for the "Street Soccer Team." He had an honest face - I'm still searching for him!

The "humisha" is the trunk of a tall palm tree. Erected to celebrate carnival, it sits in a large bucket and is adorned at the top with dozens of gifts. "Humishas" are strategically placed at the end of most streets and each "humisha tree" symbolizes the relationship between earthly man and the water kingdom. At the pre-ordained time the 'humisha" is felled and the people scramble to retrieve the gifts. I soon realized that there was status attributed to the "humisha tree". Neighbors in the better streets of town raised taller "humishas" with more expensive

gifts. Some streets had two "humishas" while others had none! I imagined a "Beverley Hills Humisha Tree" adorned with diamond bracelets, and Rolex watches.

The basic festivities stretch over a period of a week, reaching fever-pitch on Carnival Day. There are street Aquatic Parades. Communities select a water princess who parades around town on a flower-adorned float carried by young athletic-looking men. People with painted faces swarm into the Plaza de Armas throwing globos at each other. The "globos" are nothing more than colored balloons filled with water. As the "globo" hits its' human target, it bursts, drenching its' victim. By Sunday it seemed like everyone was throwing water at everybody. Youths perched in trees would hurl globos at passers-by. People were driving around town in moto-taxis carrying dozens of "globos" ready to hurl at the unlucky bystander. Neighbors stood at street corners poised with buckets of water ready to launch at a moments notice. Children would act as scouts looking for unsuspecting victims, alerting the "bucketeers" around the corner. Friends visiting my house arrived drenched, looking for dry clothes. It was a war zone!

I thought-back to those "Wet-Tee-shirt" nights at a local bar in Huntington Beach, California. Partially-clad young women wearing tee-shirts would sit on the bar to be sprayed with water droplets and the odd glass of beer. Their drenched clothing would cling to their oversized breasts leaving nothing to the imagination! People paid big bucks just to enter. Beers were at premium prices. Bouncers surrounded the female participants, ready to handcuff and arrest anyone who dared to touch or fondle them.

Workers erected an "humisha tree" directly in front of my house. The music started-up around midday and continued throughout the afternoon. Neighbors beckoned me to join-in, dragging me into their midst, as they danced around the "humisha tree". Onlookers sprayed water on me in keeping with local traditions. For a fleeting moment it felt like I was dancing around the "Maypole", an ancient English custom. On the first day of May, young eligible maidens would dance around a pole to be greeted by young eager males. It was a civilized form of a tribal mating ceremony. They wore clothes! But this after-all was the Amazon, and Iquitos stands at the center of the river communities that surround it. The water festivities are very much a central element of the local peoples' very existence.

Suddenly the dancing got faster as they played the "pandilla", a special type of erotic carnival music originating high in the Andes. A young lady smothered my face with blue dye as an elderly man rubbed Amazon mud-clay into my bald scalp. I was hit by a barrage of "globos", my pants were wet and slippery as young women (and young men) brushed-up against me, frantically dancing around the "humisha tree" to the rhythm of the "Pandilla". (Forty years in California and I hardly knew my neighbors!)

As the music intensified dancers pulsated and gyrated. Their shiny, wet-slippery bodies became enmeshed with each other, and with me! I felt like I really belonged here. I was losing control, it was wonderful! I looked around for the bouncers with handcuffs or a hidden camera. I was getting giddy dancing around the humisha as neighbors threw more "globos' and other onlookers joined the dance pressing their wet bodies up-against me. The water was so cold but I was getting so hot! So this is what they do when they can't afford Viagra!

A man, covered from head to toe in white Amazon mud-clay, joined-in the fray waving a machete. Dancers paraded behind him as he took swipes at the base of the tree. Dancers took turns with the machete, carving a series of notches until finally the moment arrived. There were loud screams as the humisha crashed to the ground and participants rushed over to the felled humisha, scrambling to grab whatever gift they could find. Fights and squabbles erupted. Sales-day at Walmart? Slowly the street returned to normal. City workers arrived to drag-off what remained of the humisha and the sun dried-out the muddy dance-puddles. Who cares about "Wet Tee-shirt Night", the "Maypole" or the "Street Soccer Team?" I'm so glad I contributed to the "Street Humisha Fund." I would hate to have missed-out on that party! I would be more than happy to contribute again next year, or next week if they wished!

Private Investigator

Barry Seymour Brett

My jungle house was under construction. Sleeping in a partially completed room, I awoke early to the crowing of the neighbor's cockerel. Stepping-over cement bags in the corridor, I slipped-into my bathroom robe and opened the restroom door. Wow! Something was missing! Whatever happened to my toilet, my commode! It was there the night before. I had occasion to use it. Several occasions! Now it was gone. The Premium model, imported from Brazil with the double-flushing action and imitation gold handle. Miguel had assured me that it was firmly cemented into the ground, but now there's just a gaping hole! That scoundrel. I knew he wasn't to be trusted. The Master-Builder, Ernesto, had recommended him to me. Now what am I to do? Good thing I had that large funnel stashed away for emergencies. You never know when they're going to come in handy! Funnels are slippery things! Why don't they sell them with handles?

Catching a mototaxi over to Ernesto's house I passed a sign advertising cement at 28 Soles a bag. But I'd been paying Ernesto 30 Soles for the same brand. Feeling ripped-off I arrived at Ernesto's house in a foul mood. "Your friend Miguel stole my toilet, the one with the gold handle" I shouted. "Don't accuse my brother-in-law of theft" he shouted-back. Brother-in-Law! Brother-in Law? Now I get the picture. This is brewing-up into a family conspiracy I thought. "Well, and what about the price of a bag of cement?" I replied in my low-grade Spanish. "That price is the dock-price he retorted. It doesn't include transportation to your house." I was caught off-guard. I really had no evidence on Miguel either. He just looked like he could have done it. After-all he was the "cement man."

"Don't worry Barry; we'll get to the bottom of this." Ernesto replied, lowering his voice in a self-assuring manner. "I know a private investigator. We could hire him." "He charges a low price and does a good job. He's a neighbor and a good friend (another brother-in-law?)." I hesitated for a brief moment. A private investigator in Iquitos? Ernesto assured me his friend had an excellent track-record and had solved many neighborhood cases. This was the man for the job.

It was ten in the morning and no sign of the nine-o'clock appointment with the "Private Investigator". A short time later Ernesto arrived on his motorbike. The Investigator had been delayed. Working on an urgent case he wouldn't be arriving until late afternoon. What could be more urgent than a missing commode I wondered? After all I could only wait so-long! Early afternoon. A knock at the door. It's Ernesto standing next to his friend (brother-in-law?) - investigator. But where was the suit, the trilby-hat cocked to the side. The dark glasses? He looked like one of those Saturday night vendors selling snake-oil on the boulevard! Very smart, I thought. He's an "under-cover man." This guy wants to blend into the surrounding neighborhood, hunting-down the perpetrator.

We sat-down at the table in my half-completed living-room. First there was the question of his fee. It would be $10 for the initial consultation and then as the investigation progressed additional expenses would be incurred. For $30 up-front he could guarantee a top quality investigation that would be completed that day and the "case solved!" A guarantee? The case solved! So I've been fooled all these years! And to think, I really believed in the FBI!

I opted for the top-quality investigation and like a magician pulling a rabbit out of a hat, out-popped the tools of the trade. Tarot Cards! No microscopic analysis or retina eye-scans with this guy. Straight to the nitty-gritty - Tarot Cards! On request, I removed my ring while he searched for the energy levels in my hand. Spreading the cards across the table he announced his preliminary finding. The thief was someone I knew. A friend, maybe a neighbor. "I knew it!" "So it was Miguel, he wasn't to be trusted." Why was I so blind? The threatening way he shook that cement trowel. It was a dead give-away. Where was my head at?

A quick shuffle and the cards revealed the gender of the suspect. It was a women, a female! "Good god, a female!" "So Miguel dresses as a woman at night!" "He's a cross-dresser. A drag Queen!" He sure didn't look like one, carrying those heavy bags of cement on his shoulder. I would never have known. The investigation intensified. The thief was a mother with young children. "A Mother!" So that's it!" "Now I get it. Miguel is really a woman in disguise!" Why didn't I think of that before? It all makes perfect sense. After-all, who would hire a women to carry cement bags?

The investigation took a sharp-turn. The thief was my next-door neighbor. Oh-well, that ruled-out Miguel. An additional fee of $5 was all it would take to complete the investigation and reveal the motive behind the theft! As I slapped-down my $5 the cards were shuffled for the final time. Yes it was definitely my neighbor and it was done for spite, not for monetary gain. "How low can you get" I thought. Steel someone's toilet for spite! That's a hit below the belt! With the forensic analysis complete, and the fees paid, my private investigator left.

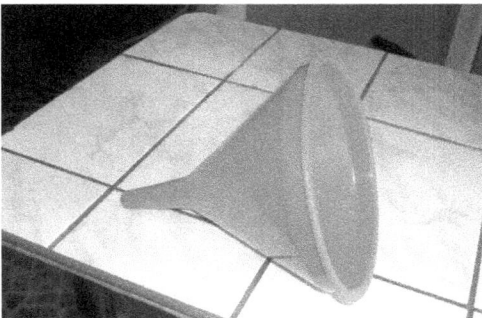

Slippery when Wet. For emergency use only. Handle with extreme care

I thought about that day in Huntington Beach, California, when someone (My son's best friend. The boy with the Christian cross dangling around his neck and the Jesus tattoo on his arm - that boy) broke into our house and stole my television. Police dusted the shelf for fingerprints. Squad cars arrived, neighbors were subjected to background checks and local pawn shops were raided as they searched in vain for my missing TV. Not even an offer of a guarantee! Just some off-the-cuff remark about how difficult it was to solve that type of robbery. All that time and money wasted on DNA analysis, fingerprinting and computerized data-bases, when all they really needed was a set of Tarot cards.

Two weeks later and there was still no sign of the replacement Brazilian commode, or my ring! Now I had to hire an investigator to investigate the investigator! Rushing across the street at a moments notice, I had to rely on the generosity of neighbors and friends. To think I thought it was Miguel. So it was my neighbor. That's why she's not talking to me anymore. Pangs of guilt every-time she pushes down the imitation gold handle! Not to worry, I lost one neighborhood friend only to find a new one. The funnel!

Death on a Rooftop

Barry Seymour Brett

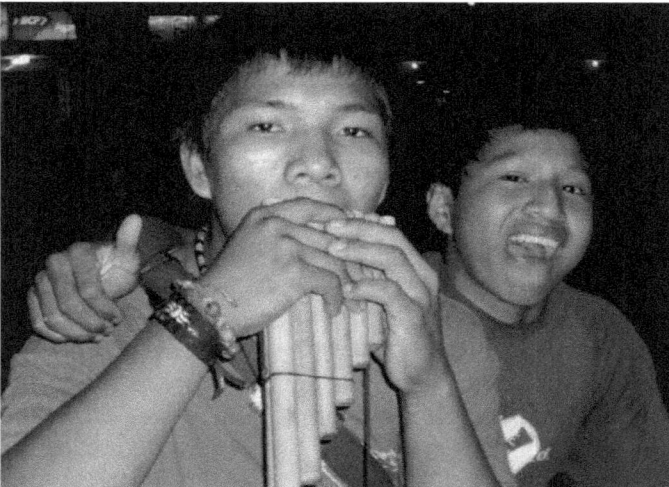

Alex on the wall playing zamponya with a friend

It was a pleasant evening. Walking along the Amazon Boulevard I stopped for an ice cream cone and glass of Inca Cola. The clowns were performing in the pit, and artisans were displaying their handicrafts as Latin dance music blasted-out from several bars and pedestrians arrived for a night on the town. For a short time I practiced my Spanish with Julio and Michael, teenage sons of my Belen friends. Julio was joined by Alex and for a while we all sat on the wall. Alex showed-off a BMX bike, a gift from a Christian Missionary passing through. Julio, Michael and other boys took turns riding the bike while

Alex sat on the wall playing Zamponya. Suddenly the street lights flickered. A few minutes later the lights went-out, the Latin Music was silenced and the Amazon Boulevard descended into darkness. At first I thought nothing of it. Power outages are a common occurrence in Jungle Cities. At least once a week in my house, and I live only one block away from Electro Oriente, the power station!

Waiting for the power to be restored, Alex played Zamponya while Michael sat on the wall singing in total darkness. They had plenty of practice. Alex had no electricity in his house and Michael's family couldn't afford to pay. They had been without electricity for the best part of the year! Suddenly we heard loud voices as people gathered on the corner across from the wall. Some people ran-off. A few minutes later Alex's friend arrived on the BMX. "A man's been electrocuted on a roof, come-on let's go check it out."

Several blocks away a group of people gathered on the corner. Waiting in the dark for power to be restored, some neighbors shone their flashlights toward the gruesome spectacle. Caught in the barbed wire, a man's body dangled from the roof, his tongue protruding from his mouth. Two policemen stood and waited for the men from Electro-Oriente. Businesses and commercial enterprises are permitted to electrify their properties against intruders. An hour passed bye and finally the fire department showed-up with a ladder. Two firemen climbed onto the roof, examined the body and then left! In the meantime more spectators arrived. The street was swarming with people. An elderly man described how he was sitting on his porch when he saw a man climbing onto the roof. Suddenly there was a horrible blue flash, the man's hair stood on end as he fell, entangled in the barbed wire. Someone from the press arrived and took photos of the body from an adjacent building. Handing the police a propina (tip), he thanked them. "Gracias Amigos, "this is front page!"

Once power was restored, the bars down the street overflowed with onlookers. Someone started a cook-out on their porch and vendors from the Boulevard arrived, selling cigarettes and sodas. Passers-by were laughing and joking while all this time the man's body dangled from the rooftop. Parents from other streets arrived with their young children. "That's what happens when you rob and steel son". Sometime later the fire department returned with the ladder. Climbing upward they took photos and then started to leave. Someone asked the fireman how much longer before the man's body would be taken-down.

"Tomorrow at noon!" "He's not a man, the police knew him, **it's the body of a thief.** It stays-up, as an example to others!"

I thought back to that grisly gang-shooting in front of my apartment in Anaheim, California. Police rushed-over to the bullet-ridden body dangling from the security gate, covering it with a blanket and hiding it from view. Relatives of the "victim" arriving at the scene were treated like royalty, even though the Cops knew full well that the whole family were drug dealing gangsters. No-one was celebrating in the streets, organizing cook-outs from their balcony or selling sodas and cigarettes, although everyone in the neighborhood was glad to get rid of him. What example did it really set I wondered? What kind of society do Californians live in when we pretend to show compassion and sorrow for a total loser and his gangster family, hiding all our blemishes and imperfections beneath a blanket?

A few days later I invited some of Alex's friends to a hot-dog party. Listening to Latin music and dancing everyone had a good time. After they left I went to take a shower. But my bar of soap, it was missing, and my toothpaste? Not the first time either, in a city of such great poverty. I thought-back to the words of the fireman. He's not a man; it's the body of a "THIEF". "I glanced upward toward my living room lights. Not even a slight flicker!

Pampachica

The Watering Hole

Barry Seymour Brett

Beachgoers waiting to cross the Nanay River for Pampachica

It was a hot, four degrees off the equator! Summertime in Iquitos. Friends suggested we visit the local watering hole. We could have gone to the "Enchanted Lagoon" or "Quistacocha". They were the preferred resorts. Pampachica, on the far-side of the Nanay River was difficult to access. It was frequented by rowdy youths looking for fun and a chance to bathe on a hot summer's day. It was the ONLY place to be!

As we approached the beachhead, I could see a flotilla of small craft resembling the Spanish Armada, carrying eager passengers to the other side. As we crossed the River Nanay, the waters reflected and amplified the music of the discotheques on the far side. It was a wild party. The beach had been underwater for more than four months, but now at last, summer had arrived and more than three thousand beach-lovers swarmed along the shoreline. The River Amazon and its' tributaries had fallen some forty feet revealing a sandy beach, perfect for a day-out with the family or friends.

One of dozens of small boats, our overloaded craft pulled into the shore. There was an overwhelming sense of excitement as everybody rushed-off the boat onto the sand. People pushed and shoved as they tried to balance themselves on the gang-plank.

Along the shoreline were hundreds of families bathing with their children. Marquees were set-up and numerous makeshift stands sold sodas and traditional foods. BBQs smoked-up the horizon. There were soccer fields and softball nets where just a few weeks earlier there had been nothing but water! The main attractions for most of the youths were the discotheques that livened-up the shoreline. Both on the beach, but especially in the discotheques, there were an overwhelmingly large number of guys and few gals. Families encourage the females to stay at home. This was especially true at Pampachica where there had been numerous incidents of robbery and assault. To an outsider it would seem strange at first, so many guys dancing with other boys. Culture shock. But no-body seemed to care. The girls didn't care either. Groups of boys would dance with each other around beer bottles strategically placed on the floor. It was all about dancing, drinking and having a good time.

At Pampachica, and especially at Street Fiestas and College dances, groups of jungle boys would sometimes dance in a circle. Every now and then different boys would take turns jumping into the center and dancing effeminately, competing with each other as they tried to imitate a girl. Boys in the circle would clap approvingly and take turns dancing with him! Sometimes a girl dancing nearby would break-through the circle of boys and dance with the impersonator! This would never happen in the U.S. or Europe, probably not even in a gay bar.

We in the West have so many hang-ups about sex and having fun. North Americans and Europeans, see a dance as an opportunity, an excuse to get close to someone of the opposite sex. Someone who, because of their hang-ups, they wouldn't normally touch, embrace or kiss in any other setting. Go to any dance in London or Los Angeles and what do you see? Most the guys never dance! They can't even break through the psychological barrier. The only reason they went to the dance was to try and meet someone to take home. They were never there to dance in the first place!

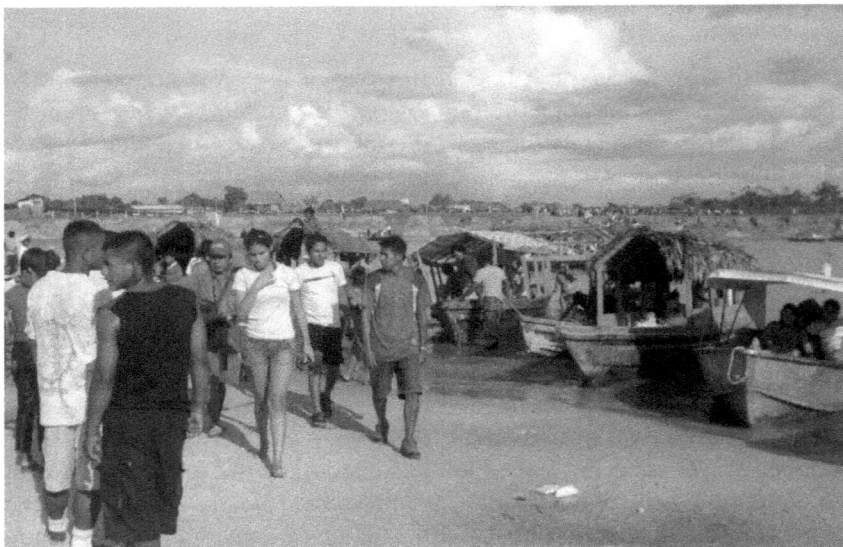
Arriving at the Watering Hole

Pampachica Vendors at the Shoreline

!

Rainforest kids have none of our hang-ups and inhibitions. Out of all the jungle dances I've attended, and there have been many, not once did I overhear a youth saying he or she planned on finding someone to hook-up with. Nor did I ever see anyone leave with someone they had first met at the dance! At a jungle dance almost EVERYONE dances, young and old. They're not on a guilt trip, looking for an excuse to get close to anyone. Jungle kids don't need to. They touch and hug each other all day long, combing each other's hair, singing and bathing together in small groups. Boys dance with boys, girls dance with girls and youths dance with partners two or three times their age because they are **not looking for anything else**. They are out to DANCE and nothing else matters to them.

There were three shore-side discotheques blasting-out "Musica Ambiente", the latest dance craze. They were packed solid with young men and women dancing, singing and drinking. There was a splattering of adults and some grandparents. All the money was made on the booze. None of the discotheques had a bathroom. Dancers wandered-over to the trees and thick foliage beyond. It was hot and humid and the dances peeked in a frenzy of excitement. Bodies were dripping with sweat but the dancing never ceased. There was no charge for entry. People in California would pay top-dollar for a sauna like this I thought. "Turn the thermostat up babe; I need to lose another ten pounds"

There were empty beer bottles and beer cases all over the dance floor. People danced around them, worshipping the Goddess of empty bottles in the vain hope that somehow, she would magically fill-up again! There was status at stake. Two beer-cases stacked on top of each other indicated real partiers with cash. Dancing around a lone beer bottle was not good for one's image! Frowned-upon. Good looking chicks, in heavy demand, would pass-on-by.

The most popular drink "Climax", an alcoholic carbonated soda, was sold in two-liter bottles. The more affluent dancers would mix it with beer to give it an extra "Kick!" No drinking age limit was enforced. How could it be? Most the kids had no I.D. and no chance of ever getting one. Why? They were born in odd-ball villages, two or three days down-river from the nearest town. They never had a birth certificate to begin with and will never be able to get one! If there were an age limit, who would enforce it? Three or four thousand beach-goers at Pampachica, and not even one cop.

My friends wanted to dance. Dripping with perspiration and gyrating to "Daddy Yankee" and "Porn Lust" I lost my step and committed the cardinal crime. There it was, all spilled-out across the dance-floor. Like blood from a sacrificial cow. Someone's beer! I'd kicked-over the Goddess! For a moment I froze as the beer bottle-worshipper approached, his "Terminator Body" scanning the horizon looking for the "Spiller!" I felt his red laser-beam lock-onto-target. Lost for words, I struggled to understand his Spanish. No time to pull-out my "Easy Spanish Phrase Book" I thought. What good would it do anyway; I could read the expression on his face in "English!" Two simple words; "Pay-back!" Lucky-break. Just as he was about to stab me with those liquid-metal stabbing devices, his friends pulled him away from the brink! I ran to the beach looking for Arnold. He could save me! No such luck, he was in Sacramento, California, hiding from taxpayers in the Governor's Mansion! It was time to leave!

It was getting dark. Crossing to the far-shore in a small craft, I noticed that nobody was sober, including the Captain and crew. Passengers were singing and drinking. Desperately trying to illuminate the surrounding waters, the Captain held a small flashlight. Where was his compass? I guess he traded-it-in for a bottle of rum! We seemed to go round in circles that quickly became a spiral. No-one cared! A ten-minute cruise became a forty minute circum-navigation of the globe. When we finally docked we were miles downstream and nowhere near the beachhead. "So this is how Columbus discovered America!"

A motokaro dropped-us-off in the Plaza de Armas. Smack in the center of Iquitos. I walked past the bars on the Amazon Boulevard, but now they all looked so civilized and boring. A friend hailed me over to his table. "Hi Barry, I hear you went to Pampachica" I looked at the neatly-stacked empty beer bottles as the soothing music of "Love Ballad" wafted in the background. But "Love Ballad" didn't cut it anymore. I yearned to return to the watering hole; to the excitement and ambience of "Pampachica". The flashing lights and screams of hysteria, the sheer electricity generated by hundreds of bodies pulsating to the rhythm of "Porn Lust" and "Daddy Yankee". "Barry, let's kick-back, relax, have a quiet beer and enjoy the evening!!" - No Way.

Barrio Florido

Barry Seymour Brett

Bars leading down to the Port of Nanay

The Port of Nanay. There was a small square in the center of town. It was summertime and a street lined with bars led down to the waterfront. During the winter the river rises and the waterfront meets the main square! At the far-end of the street were a few dozen boats waiting to take passengers downriver to remote Amazonian villages. Some were rowing boats and others were the notorious "pecky-peckys", named after the sound they make as they ply the streams and rivers. I was traveling with my neighbor's son, Ricardo. As several boatmen pushed and shoved trying to gain our attention, Antonio walked us over to the small boat. "This is my brother Colombo (Columbus)". Oh well, we won't get lost with him I thought. There he was, Colombo the "Pecky-pecky man, pulling the cord frantically trying to start the motor. Twenty pulls later and still no "Peck". I had a spinning-top like that once. After about seven or eight pulls on the cord, finally it would rotate with that humming sound. But my top didn't need gasoline! Did we mind paying-up-front for the trip? Gasoline costs money!!

Thirty minutes and one gas-can later and we were on our way. It was a two hour boat ride to Barrio Florido, a small pueblo (village) on the River Amazon. My friend Howard and his younger brother Juan had invited me to spend the night there. I would meet his parents, his sister and aunt and we would all go visit the local discotheque. Finally we docked at Barrio Florido. As Ricardo led me down the small street to the center of town, we passed men carrying bananas back toward the dock. Howard and Juan came running-up to greet us. Howard's parents had the only phone in the pueblo (village). He had a small rowing boat and he would row us over to his Aunt's house for dinner. On the way over we passed the oil refinery. "Petro-Peru", the refiner of liquid gold. One of a handful of successful companies making money in the Amazon. Yes there's oil under the ground, deep in the rainforest.

After dinner at his Aunt's house, Howard took us over to the little discotheque. The pride of the pueblo. The run-down wooden shack would surely make the Guinness Book of Records as the smallest discotheque in the world. It reminded me of Grandma's outhouse! It had a small lamp dangling from a cord and every now and then flashes of sunlight would flicker through the cracks in the wooden wall. There was a gaping hole on one side next to a wooden bench. Not exactly my idea of a discotheque I thought as I searched for an excuse to leave. At least I felt good after I left Grandma's outhouse!

Howard, Ricardo and Juan played soccer in the street with the local kids for a while and then we visited some of their friends. In the evening we returned to the tiny discotheque. Ricardo introduced me to Rosa and Maria. They wanted to dance. Maria's brothers would play drums "Amazon Style", while Howard's neighbor would sing and play Zamponya. A young boy arrived carrying a rain-stick (hollow bamboo filled with jungle seeds). He would thump-out a rhythm on a wooden box as an elderly man shook the rainstick. Within minutes the whole village showed-up. Colombo, (back from his "discovery!"), handed me a bottle of home-brewed liquor distilled from Amazon root plants. The music got faster and the steady beat of the washboard and jungle drums intensified drowning-out the sweet sound of the Zamponya. Jungle girls with athletic bodies climbed all over me as young guys joined in the fray.

Pouring beer into "Climax", an alcoholic carbonated soda, Ricardo handed me "El Submarino." Howard's sister gave me a sip of her "Trago Especial" (special mixture), more commonly referred to as "Sex in the Jungle". Young men lifted me onto their shoulders and paraded me around the small room while beautiful young ladies caressed my body and massaged my bald head. "I'm ready now" Howard's sister whispered in my ear, as she took another sip of the "Trago Especial." "Oh, really, ready for what?" To dance, or maybe? "Oh,- that!" My whole body vibrated as I twisted and turned, dancing wildly to the sound of the Amazon jungle drums.

"La Energia de la Selva" (The Energy of the Jungle) engulfed me as more villagers arrived and the party and dancing spilled-out into the street. Someone set-up a home-brewed wine stand out-front as young boys waited patiently, ready to carry their parents and older brothers back home. Two sips of the jungle wine and I found myself staggering across the room searching for the bathroom. Young girls above me danced on the wooden bench. Gyrating and pulsating to the steady beet of the jungle drums and washboard, they lured me into their midst. Swigging on "submarinos," young men pressed-up against them, massaging their beautiful jungle bodies in rhythm with the washboard. Grandma's outhouse was "NEVER" like this!! I began to wonder if we really needed all those electronic strobe lights and multi-colored plasma displays. Suddenly I saw them as nothing less than a distraction.

Howard and Ricardo helped carry me back to the house. The following morning as we wandered back-down to the dock, Howard asked me when I would be coming-back to Barrio Florido. "Well, not for a few weeks". "Barry, don't come on Wednesday again." "If you really want some fun, come on Friday or Saturday. The discotheque really rocks at weekends!

There was one large boat to Nanay waiting at the landing. The "Elegante" (Elegant). Men were loading bananas as we finally got ready to leave. Halfway back to Nanay and suddenly smoke came bellowing out of the hold as we came to a complete stop. The smoke engulfed the cabins and lower deck as passengers scrambled up-top. Having sold the radio for gasoline the Captain would wave-down a "passing vessel". Why don't we send-out "smoke signals" I thought! It was getting dark and still no vessel "passed!" I began to wish we had sails. I looked below deck for the oarsmen chained to the floor and the

Centurion with the mallet. They could help us. "Battle Speed", Collision Speed!"

It was daybreak when finally a boat appeared on the horizon. Our Captain waved and shouted. Overloaded with bananas they refused to help unless we paid them an outrageous sum.. Late afternoon and still no help. But what's that sound in the distance? "Peck-peck, Peck-peck". It was our old friend "Colombo" again, navigating the world in his pecky-pecky. He would take us back to Nanay for free! As we pulled into Nanay I noticed Colombo searching under the seats for something. The gas can. "And by-the-way, do you think you could fill-it up?"

As I rode home from Nanay in a motokaro I thought for a moment about my late Grandma. God bless her soul. She was a wild thing, she was. Grandma would have loved to dance on the wooden bench at Barrio Florido. To think she had a discotheque right there in her backyard all those years, and yet she didn't know it!

Monkey Wars

Barry Seymour Brett

Displaying red war paint, one of several Red Uakari Monkeys sitting on a hayawasca branch and preparing to attack!

It was a warm pleasant morning as we prepared to sail down-river in the "Dawn on the Amazon", one of several boats owned by my good friend Captain Bill Grimes. Leaving from the small port of Nanay we sailed up-river for an hour or so, finally arriving at the tiny pueblo (town) of Padre Cocha. I had visited the pueblo four years earlier and not surprisingly nothing had changed.

Tool-using Black Capuchin battle monkey

Traveling with another Californian and his eight year old son, Antonio, we walked a mile or so along narrow pathways eventually arriving at a junction. A makeshift board illustrated with colorful butterflies beckoned us to a small clearing where a large sign warned against using cameras with flash. Taking flash-pictures of the warning we proceeded across a rickety bridge to the "Butterfly Farm" entrance.

As we approached the entrance several monkeys ambushed us from adjacent trees. Trying to steal my "Lakers" baseball cap and Antonio's sunglasses they followed us to a seating area in front of the reception office. As we sat down, other visitors joined us. It was a trap! Monkeys clung to our backs, and sat on our shoulders. One of the spiteful little red ones frantically tried to tie my shoes together. It was a war zone. One of the red monkeys appeared to be suffering from an epileptic fit. Initiated by an intense camera flash, she lay on the ground, limbs flailing about. Squealing, crying, quivering she reminded me of my ex-wife when she couldn't get her own way! Offered some bananas and other monkey-goodies, suddenly, miraculously, that nasty little monkey snapped out of the fit and just like my wife, resumed normalcy! My credit card and a trip to the mall would bring my wife out of her self-induced coma. That's all it would take. And she took it all! No bananas and nuts for my gal!

Angry that someone had used a flash camera, Gudrun, the owner of the "Butterfly Farm", rushed-over to attend to the monkey. A wonderful lady, absolutely devoted to jungle wild life, she nevertheless has little sympathy for the plight of us humans! We humans are no more than simple-minded pets. Gudrun and her ilk will never rest until all humans are caged and all wild-life is freed from captivity!

There were several species of monkey prancing and jumping between the trees. The majority were red-faced Uakari monkeys and the more aggressive black Capuchin monkeys. The Capuchin monkeys stole the show. Intelligent tool-users, the Capuchin monkeys were always searching for odd jobs knocking nails into coconuts. The Capuchins suspected the red-faced Uakari's of working for less than the minimum wage of three bananas a day! There was no love lost between them. Constantly threatening each other with hisses and tooth displays it was like a London Pub after the game! All species of monkey were envious and jealous of their human rivals. Occupying just one small branch on the evolutionary tree, they yearned for the day man would become extinct and a monkey could sit on the top. Monkeys would pretend to pose for photo-ops and then jump aggressively at defenseless humans. Not satisfied with threatening gestures they would cling to the legs of innocent bystanders. Sensing man's most vulnerable point, they would attempt to steal his wallet and camera, thereby ruining his vacation and delivering an almost fatal blow. Wanting to release their Chimpanzee cousins from captivity, they would put their tiny hands into people's pockets, desperately searching for passports, frequent flyer discounts and roundtrip air tickets to San Diego.

Then suddenly there it was. Every parent's worst nightmare. The primordial scream of a human child. On the verge of extinction by global warming (or cooling), a poor little defenseless human boy cried-out in pain. Viciously attacked and bitten by battle-monkeys this young boy was about to be put on the endangered species list at the Ana Stahl Clinic. Once the boat returned to Iquitos, he would require a series of excruciatingly painful rabies shots spread over three days. Eco-tourists looked-on in total disbelief. How was it possible? Why would a "wild animal" attack a peace-loving child? Surely if we don't interfere with wild animals and their way of life, if we leave them alone and don't take sides, don't threaten them or try to impose our values on them, just surrender to them and give them everything they want, then surely they won't attack us! How could this have happened? He was just an innocent child! He wasn't wearing a military uniform, waving the Stars & Stripes, or carrying a bomb? His dad didn't work for the CIA or Animal Control! In a split second everything they had come to believe in was shattered by a bite.

Following some temporary medical treatment for the boy's hand, the tour resumed. For a while we all petted Rosa the giant anteater, before visiting Pedro Bello, the caged Jaguar. A splendid beast, he had been in captivity for most of his life. As the helper pushed a clump of meat through the wire netting, I wondered exactly who was a threat to whom! Grabbing the meat with his large jaw, Pedro proceeded to sit down in front of us, roaring and glaring at us with his giant head and massive teeth. Gudrun had assured me that this magnificent beast was on the verge of extinction. Why then did she spend $10,000 building a metal fence and installing wire-netting to protect "us" from him? He watched as we proceeded to entertain him with our cabaret acts. We made comments about the massive teeth, stupendous black and yellow skin and long sharp claws. He'd heard it all one thousand times before. This magnificent cat was subjected once again to the sight of a small group of weak pathetic humans standing before him. Those peeping toms, protected by a wire fence, would take his picture without permission and brag to their California friends and relatives about their wild-life encounter! But inside, deep down inside, he always knows. One lunge, one jump and the table turns. Victim becomes victor.

Returning to the pueblo we boarded the boat and took a trip upriver to visit the Boa tribe. They were interesting people. Kind and friendly but nevertheless ruthless when it came to conducting business. Any sign of weakness was exploited and they could certainly drive a hard bargain. Tribesman competed with poison dart blowguns. Missiles would hit on target from over fifty feet away. Wearing tribal paint they danced with rain sticks to music dating all the way back to the ancient Incas. Visitors were encouraged, pressured into painting their faces. They were then expected to join in the dancing and to wear the dance-paint and feather headdress. Antonio, the young Californian boy, his hand still in pain, nevertheless joined in the dancing with his dad. There were dozens of handicrafts on wall displays throughout the large hut. Paintings of jungle life, handbags and wallets made from armadillos, tree bark and crocodiles. Large frightening tribal masks, skulls and poison dart blowguns.

Seven year-old kids tying-up the "Dawn on the Amazon" boat

Walking back toward the "Dawn on the Amazon" we met the two seven year olds who had tied-up our boat and had been guarding it for us. Before walking up the gangplank, Antonio the California boy showed-off the souvenir he had just bought from the tribal chief. Opening-up the plastic bag as the two kids looked-on; he pulled-out the large handmade necklace and placed it around his neck. There it was, strung with beads made from jungle seeds and embellished with brightly colored feathers. Pay-back; a Monkey Skull!

Antonio Cordova, bite victim, displaying his trophy

Flash picture of the "No-Flash" sign

Rosa the Giant Anteater enjoying lunch

A Rose is but a Rose

Barry Seymour Brett

"What's in a name? That which we call a Rose, by any other name would smell as sweet."

Romeo & Juliet; William Shakespeare (The Balcony Scene)

I hadn't been in the city more than a few hours. Walking across the Plaza de Armas toward the Amazon Boulevard someone selling trinkets yelled-out to me "Pelacho". I thought nothing of it. Later, in front of the movie-theatre I heard it again. "Pelacho". Were they talking to me? I thumbed thru my "Berlitz - Spanish in Ten Minutes" Nothing there. Back at the hotel a waiter told me that it was a vulgar form of "Bald one!" "Oh, I get it" (Bald S.O.B.) "Oh yes, really? That's the end of your tip buddy." "I'll never sit at your table again." Ever since my chemotherapy I've been sensitive about my hair-loss. I nurtured the last remaining strand. Pampering it, trailing-it as it wound its way around my head. Then there was that awful morning when I woke-up, only to find it lying on the pillow next to me. I lovingly placed it in a sealed plastic bag. I felt naked without it. I even thought about gluing-it back-on!

There're some nasty people in this town I thought. "Straight to my face", not even the decency to call me names behind my back! Three teenagers - safety in numbers. Well, this bald S.O.B. can still kick some you know what I thought, as I imagined myself hitting them over the head with a club. After all, I won the "Whack-a-Mole" contest at Chucky Cheese's Pizza House. I was the champion. My Son told me! Later that day while attempting to get directions to a local discotheque, a man blurted-out "Chato" across the street to his friend. There it was, in the dictionary at the back of my "What they never taught you at school - Street Spanish Phrase Book". "Short-one! (That's being kind)" At a local bar a young teenager yelled-out "Chino" to attract the barman's attention. I didn't need a dictionary for that one. He looked like he'd just left the doctor's office after a bad dose of Lasik eye surgery. You know. The two for the price of one deal by that "Out-of-State" surgeon! They don't get any narrower than that I thought.

At a fiesta a few days later, my young friend introduced me to his neighbor. "Hey, Alto," (tall-one) he screamed, as his friend wandered-over, bumping his head against the Piñata. Dancing to a popular Lima group, "Dilbert Aguilar", my friend asked me if I liked 'Dwarf Music!" Well, there's that song, "Hey ho, hey ho its home from work we go." But he wasn't talking about "Snow White". The lead-singer was "height-challenged!" Her Majesty, the Queen of England was La Reina Viejita Blanca (The Old White Queen). Mirror, Mirror on the Wall, who is the fairest of them all? "The Old White Queen!" She sounded like something on a chess board! Have they no respect at all? Didn't they realize that they were talking about Her Royal Imperial Highness? The richest woman in the World! (Sorry Oprah Winfrey - but you just don't cut-it!). A young "hearing-impaired" man who hovered outside restaurants looking for table-leftovers was always called "Mute". Good thing he couldn't hear what people called him I thought. In this topsy-turvy world there were no "amputees" or "handicapped", only "cripples. The "welfare-challenged?" Well no two words about it, they were just plain beggars. Then there was my friend who sold cigarettes on the street corner. Everybody called him Gordo (Fat-one) - even his Mother!

When people didn't want to shout abusive names at each other they could always whistle. I never was much of a whistler myself. If I was meant to whistle I would have been born with a beak! But this is the jungle and I soon noticed that young men and women in Iquitos could imitate all kinds of jungle bird sounds. My ex-wife was good at that. She squawked a lot! Especially in the divorce court. The judge must have been a bird-lover. He gave her everything!

There was a "Whistling Morse-Code" of the jungle. Attempting to attract a street vendor's attention, customers would whistle loudly. Vendors knew what the whistle meant. There were screechy whistles that signified urgency. Sudden double-bursts that meant "Why are you ignoring me" and the classic "shrill'. "Hey Buddy, I'm over here". To create the "Shrill" young men would stick both fingers in their mouths, stretching their lips halfway around their heads. But don't let's forget the "oodle!" The tongue vibrates wildly as both fingers are pushed deep into the throat like they're reaching into "Santa's Christmas Stocking". If whistling wasn't your bag, you could always use the hand-signs. The classic U.S. hand-sign for "give me a call" meant "let's go have a beer" when it was used with both hands moving rapidly toward the mouth. A fist hammering into the hand meant "Plata" (money)" A fist thrust directly into the palm with a loud smack meant only one thing. Yes, that!

I soon discovered that teenagers hanging-out on the Boulevard had street names. Looking for Michael, a friend reminded me that he was known as "La Gallina" (the hen). Oscar was always called "Mala Suerte" (bad-luck). After my shoes and baseball cap went missing I found-out why! The one with the limp was (hoppy) and the boy with acne was (spotty). The teenager, Robinson, who sold popsicles, was known only as "Muerto" (dead-one). Then there was "Juevo" (Egg). I asked a friend why he was always called "Egg", even by his parents and older brother. "Oh Barry, you just don't get it" "He's got one missing!" A soccer player, they'll be calling him "Omelet" next! Girls? Well there was (breasty and preggy) and La Facilita (the easy one!).

Slowly I began to piece-it-together. It's us! We are the ones that have it all wrong. We in the rich West are living a lie. If you're fat, then you're fat. Why go around pretending otherwise. Nobody in Iquitos seemed to be offended by those remarks. Everyone just took it in their stride and went about their daily business.

Back in the U.S., driving down the Golden State Freeway with my neighbor, I turned-on the car stereo. There it was. "Nigger". That popular reggae ton group from South America. With two huge hits they had finally made the U.S. charts. But wait a minute, something was wrong. South American bands introduce themselves at the start of the song. "This is Nigger" had been dubbed-over. The band had suffered a name change. "Nigger" was now "T.J.Flex!" I wondered why we've become so sensitive. Cats and dogs are not castrated, they're doctored. They're not killed. Just put-to-sleep, even though everyone knows they won't be waking-up anytime soon! Junkyards are recycling centers and the blind are seeing-impaired. Have we all gone mad?

Picking-up speed as we approached the four-level Hollywood Interchange, I pondered our unwillingness to face reality and call things what they were. Suddenly a driver chomping-down on a hamburger whilst clinging to his cell phone swerved around me. As I braked, my tires screeching and smoking, my neighbor wound down the window. "Get a Life - You (?)-sucking Son of a B" he screamed as he gave the finger! So there's hope for us yet!!!

Fiesta San Juan

Barry Seymour Brett

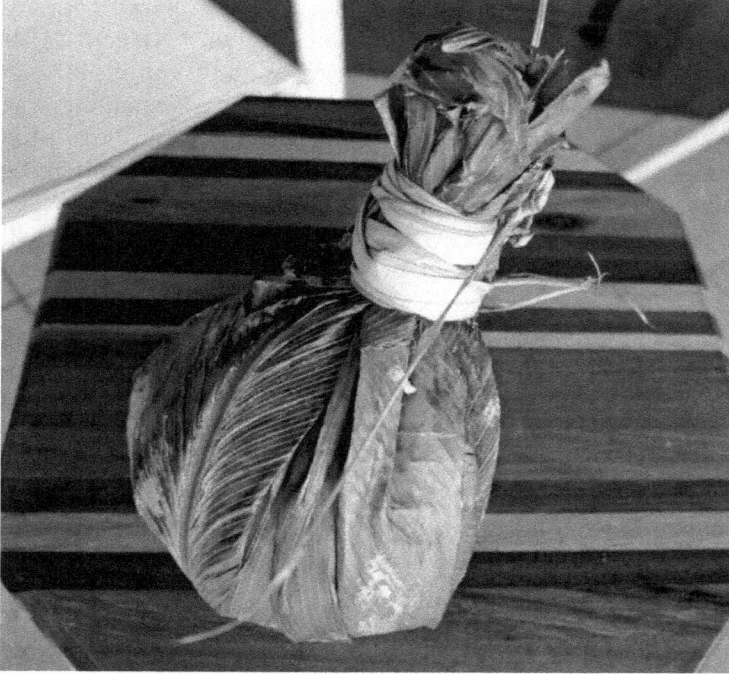

"Juane" – the "Fish & Chips"; the "Pizza" of the Rainforest

Named after "Saint John the Baptist", the patron Saint of the Amazon, San Juan sits some forty minutes away from downtown Iquitos smack in the middle of the rainforest. "Fiesta San Juan" is the biggest event on the calendar. Dozens of stands are set-up in the Plaza Roja. Thousands of villagers for miles around flock to the square to participate in the events which last for five days. People living in the more remote jungle areas set-out two or three days beforehand. Walking or canoeing, they find some way to get to San Juan to join in the celebration.

As I jumped into a motokaro in-front of my house, my neighbor yelled-out "don't forget to **have your Juane**" (pronounced Wanee).

Looking forward to the fiesta I also wanted to visit my friend Ron. He owned a house in San Juan close to the main square. The streets leading-into the city were jammed solid with people walking to the fiesta. As the taxi driver dropped me off near the Plaza Roja, he reminded me to **"have my Juane"**.

Walking down the street toward the Chinese restaurant I passed a large hall. There they were, a couple of hundred "Hill People", dancing and singing as a small band played at the far end. But what a strange sight it was to behold. Everyone was waving around handkerchiefs! There was a rhythm to it. Some women, especially the older ones, waved hand-embroidered handkerchiefs embellished with beautiful designs. Some guys waved their bandanas. There was something very sexy, seductive, and suggestive about the waving. Very crowded and hot toward the center of the dance floor, dancers were stripping-off and waving their shirts and who knows what else? Waving them about in a seductive, almost hypnotic manner, dancers engaged each other in a frenzy of excitement. I wanted to join-in but I had no handkerchief. It looked like you could wave around just about anything - No, not that!

Toward the center of the dancehall was a statuette that had seen better days. Streaks of color marred the face which was badly cracked and disfigured. "Mother-in-law!" For a brief moment I felt like smashing it to smithereens! At last a man lent me his handkerchief while he wandered over to the giant goldfish bowl!. Yes, there it was to the side of the band - punch. Or was it punch? A young lady stirred the bright red brew and handed me a glass. As I took a gulp it reminded me of transmission fluid on ice. A bystander told me they were worshipping a Saint! Maybe so, but which one? "Econo-Lube" or "Firestone Automotive!" Maybe they were worshipping mother-in-law!

Mystically waving her beautifully embroidered handkerchief in rhythm with the music, a young lady engaged me in semaphore. Hypnotizing me with her body movements and seductive waves, I felt I was falling in love. As I took another swig of the "Tranny Fluid" another good looking girl flagged me down! Frantically waving her multicolored handkerchief she seemed to be signaling something. Was it an S.O.S? "Don't dance with her, she's a tramp!" she seemed to be saying. As I looked around there he was, waving his red handkerchief at me like he was on the deck of an aircraft carrier in World War Two. "The boyfriend!" Was he challenging me? Or maybe he just wanted to give me an oil change! Red rag to a bull I thought as my handkerchief-lender returned from the "Tranny-Bowl" to re-claim his property and save my skin. Very popular amongst the hill people around Cuzco and the Bolivian border, the "Danza con Panuelo" (Handkerchief Dance) is taught at dance schools in Trujillo and Lima.

I was feeling hungry. It was time to **"Have my Juane"**. The central feature of "Fiesta San Juan" is the "Juane", the "Fish & Chips", the "Pizza" of the rainforest peoples. A ball of rice flavored with jungle root spice and olives surrounding a chunk of chicken. Wrapped and cooked in bijao palm leaves it has a very distinctive flavor. "Juanes", the staple diet of the Amazonian peoples are sold throughout the rainforest, and nowhere do they taste better than here in San Juan, their namesake. Nowhere do they cost as much either! Juanes that normally sell for one sole (30 cents) were selling for six soles ($2). It's part of the Amazonian tradition to visit San Juan at least once in your lifetime to **"Have your Juane"**.

Taking a stroll around the plaza I noticed there were dozens of vendors selling local handicrafts, hot dogs, BBQ'd meat, ice cream cones, sodas and even donuts. Yes, donuts while-you-wait. Dropping dough into a wok a young boy would fish the donuts out with a stick and smother them with syrup. There was a midway with Ferris wheels and all kinds of carnival games and rides as hundreds of people paraded along the narrow pathways between the stands. Near the main road was a discotheque blasting-out loud music across the Plaza as a multitude of kids danced and drank on the upper level. The upper balcony, vibrating and overloaded with revelers out for a good time, could have collapsed at any moment. Glancing upward I noticed the name. "Discoteka Titanica!"

Walking around the side of the "Discotheque Titanic" I could see my friend Ron's house. But wait a minute. Gosh, what are all those young men lining-up for? Ron must be throwing a party or something. That's strange; I don't recall seeing a red-light over his porch before! Something must be going-on. Ron told me to drop-by anytime I was in town. I think he must have meant anytime except today! But what's that? Surely not. Good god, there's a stripper dancing in his window! So that's what **"Having your Juane"** means!

Crossing the road to the Chinese restaurant, I bumped into my friends Arturo and Victor chomping-down on some spaghetti as a traditional street-band played zamponya, drums and flute. After dinner we walked around the square. For a while we watched the man with the shells. Which shell hid the coin? Madly switching the shells around, bets were placed. The same woman (his wife) kept betting large sums. It was a shakedown. Like a woman in a divorce court, she would always win while everyone else lost.

Then there were those rings. You know the ones I mean. Just a hair too narrow to fit over the neck of a bottle. The balls that morphed into bean-bags, crashing to the ground just before they reached their target. Dices that always landed on low numbers and spinning arrows that always pointed toward a family member or friend of the game-owner. It was a strange thing, but everyone seemed to be having such a good time being ripped-off! How were they able to steel people's money while their victims laughed and smiled? The I.R.S. would pay big bucks to discover their secret!

Two o'clock in the morning and everything was shutting-down. There were no motokaros close-by. We walked a mile or two out-of-town, finally flagging-one down. As we drove toward Iquitos we passed hundreds of fiesta-goers, many carrying young children, walking-back home. There was no public transport, and most had no money. They lost it all while they laughed and smiled. Now it would take them the best part of a year to save-up enough cash to visit "Fiesta San Juan" again to "Have their Juane".

I'm also heading back to San Juan next year to "Have my Juane." I'll be easy to spot. I'll be waving a handkerchief and carrying a dip-stick! I'm low on cash right now. I wonder where they sell those red lights?

The Shoe Story

Barry Seymour Brett

In Iquitos, Peru, a city of half a million, many people are shoeless. If they wear anything on their feet at all it would almost certainly be a pair of sandals.

Enjoying breakfast in the main square I was approached by Fernando, one of many shoeshine boys that frequented the Plaza de Armas in downtown Iquitos. He wanted to clean my shoes. Fernando had a shoebox hand-painted with beautiful jungle flora and parrots. But where was it? "This isn't your shoebox" I remarked as I glanced at the Nazi Insignia, Hammer and Sickle and painting of Che Guevera. "No this is Javier's box; I'm just borrowing it for the day." I wondered what kind of clientele Javier catered to. Exactly whose shoes was he cleaning? Goose-stepping Nazis, or maybe Colonel Klebs with those spring-loaded poison dart shoes! "I have to give it back tonight" Fernando explained, "Javier needs it for tomorrow. It's just for one day".

Someone had stolen Fernando's hand-painted shoebox. The workhorse, the engine of prosperity that brought home a trickle of money everyday. A smidgen of cash, just barely enough to feed his brothers and sisters, all nine of them! Now it was all over for them. They would go to school without food, probably for several days in a row. He would scour the trash mounds looking to salvage something edible. Life as they had known it had suddenly come to an end. "Barry you don't know what it's like to be a shoe-shine boy." "Every day I clean people's fancy expensive shoes, always knowing that as long as I live I will never be able to afford to own a pair." For a brief moment I thought about that part-time job at the Beverly Hills Car Wash. All those fancy Rolls-Royces and as long as I live I'll never be able to afford to rent one for the day, let alone own one! "Look at me" Fernando said, "These sandals are all I have. My uncle makes them from old car tires" As I picked one up I noticed the trade mark underneath. "Firestone".

A week or so later I bumped into Fernando again. But where were the new shoes I had bought him? The imitation "Nikes" made in China with Child Labor!!! He was wearing his "Firestones". "I don't get to wear my new shoes much". "Before when I had none, I borrowed my neighbors' or my cousins' shoes. Now they're taking turns wearing mine!" "But wait, I see you've got a new shoe box." "Yes, some days I rent-out my new shoes to villagers for a wedding or a funeral. I spent the money on a new shoebox." "But what's that? A naked lady painted on the side!" "Whatever happened to the beautiful jungle fauna and parrots?" "I don't care much for parrots any more Barry". "I'm twelve years old now."

Evening time. We were going to Gabriel's school a few blocks away. The school was holding a "Promotion", a fund raiser. Arriving at my house early, Gabriel wanted to know if I had any glue. Glancing down I noticed the large paper-clip holding together one of his shoes. But wait a minute. "Good gosh Carlos, those shoes are way too big". **"Girls like big shoes!"** "I borrowed them from my cousin". "He's a size 40 and I'm only 32!" "I pad them with toilet paper" he explained as I rushed to the bathroom to replace the roll. But where was Ricardo? Just as we were about to leave Ricardo arrived complete with battle wound. A black eye! "I had to fight for the shoes." "We only have one pair in the family and my older brother wanted them." "I can't go to the "Promotion" without shoes, I want to dance." And the black-eye?

There it was, "The Promotion". More than two hundred teenagers and a splattering of adults, dancing and drinking in the main hall draped with the school colors and festooned with balloons. They would dance and drink until 4am! The school group the "Dangling Trunks" was playing loud music while young female students wearing almost nothing wiggled their you-know-what on stage. There were stands to the side selling cigarettes, candies, sodas and yes, beer! Gabriel lost his paper-clip and ended-up dancing barefooted as Carlos raced to the bathroom, stuffing his big shoes with more toilet paper! A raffle was held for a soccer ball and a bottle of cheap perfume.

Some students could be seen entering the Hospedaje (rooming house) next door where rooms could be rented by the hour! Some teachers, those that could still stand, were drinking and dancing with their students. There was wild talk and student banter about which teachers were in love with which students. Fourteen and fifteen year-olds sat at the gambling table betting on card games as they blew cigarette smoke at each other whilst swigging down the booze. There was a loud cheer as the "Master of Ceremonies", somewhat the worse for booze, staggered to the ground, only to be carried-out to a waiting mototaxi by his brothers.

Prom Night at Huntington Beach High was like dancing in a graveyard compared to this. But this is the jungle, and people here know how to "live" and how to "party!" It was gone three in the morning and time to leave. But where was Carlos with his big shoes? Gabriel saw him enter the hospedaje with two young girls! Suddenly my size 42s seemed a little too tight. So that's why most the restrooms in Iquitos have no toilet paper! We would have to wait!

Californian authorities would have shut this party down in an instant. The barman would have been arrested, the school fined, the Principal fired and the "Dangling Trunks" charged with obscenity and thrown into Juvenile Hall. They would have been psychoanalyzed to find-out why their "trunks dangled" and what else was "wrong with them!" There would be an enquiry, an investigation and a lawsuit. Attorneys across the nation would be licking their greedy lips desperately trying to join in the fray. All that over a simple school dance to raise money for books!

It was midnight. We were one short as we waited patiently in the Plaza de Armas. There he was, running up to us, Angelo, the shoeshine boy. Now we had our soccer team "The Piranhas". Arriving at the brightly-lit Plaza San Antonio, we waited patiently while other teams played, waiting our chance. Team members would contribute a few pennies each to create a "pot'. Each side would play for the pot. Finally a team lost and "The Piranhas" had their chance to play against the winners. "But Barry, they're cheating" Angelo exclaimed. "There's no way we can win against them." "We should wait for another team to show-up". "But how? How are they cheating?" I asked. "Can't you see? Look Barry, look. "Some of them are wearing shoes!"

Copyright September 2009

Bar on the Amazon

Barry Seymour Brett

The Arandu Bar. One of several lining the Amazon Boulevard

I was just a tourist passing through. Like most people who visit Iquitos, Peru, I had no intentions of sticking around. Iquitos was to be no more than a stopover before heading down-river to Manaus and Rio, Brazil. The longer I stayed, the more enthralled with Iquitos I became. She was like a beautiful woman. Just when I thought I knew everything about her, out would pop a new trick. The Boulevard was the center of activity. Stretching along the banks of the River Amazon, the Boulevard boasted some of the best bars and restaurants in town. Thousands of people gathered at weekends to watch the clowns and other artists perform.

There was a splattering of foreigners living in Iquitos. Some odd-ball characters frequented the boulevard. I soon got to know Gene and Bill. Gene thought he was an FBI agent. He even carried a badge! Flashing his badge to impress a lady-friend, I recognized it instantly. My son had one. We bought it at "Toys are Us", together with the water pistol!

Bill lived in Maryland. We had something in common. I had lived in Rockville, Maryland for eight years. I knew the area well. Inheriting money from the sale of his deceased Mother's house, Bill was looking to buy "El Punto de Encuentro." A bar on the Amazon Boulevard. Bill was a musician with no business experience. I offered to help.

Sitting next to Bill, across the table from the seller, I struggled to peer-over the mountain of dollar bills stacked sky-high. Just as Bill was about to sign, his attorney arrived. "No Bill, No. Don't sign" he shouted" "This man's not the owner! The bar belongs to his ex-wife and she's on vacation in Lima!" The imposter left. It would take another week to finalize the purchase. Suddenly with little warning Bill had to leave for the States. Until he returned the bar was mine. I had managed a restaurant in Downtown Washington DC for almost two years. But this was Iquitos, Peru.

There were three regular employees. One waitress, "Rosa" and one waiter "Teodoro." "Soyla," well she was manager and ran the bar. They had worked at the bar for several years. Opening in the early afternoon there was little or no business before six or seven at night. They would pass the days watching "Spanish Soaps" on the big-screen TV. But by the end of the second month I began to realize that we had problems. The money wasn't there. We were running at a loss!

But wait. The electric bill. It was way too high. My good friend and Master-Builder Ernesto explained. "Barry, you're no-longer paying for a trickle." The main current by-passed the gauge. "The previous bills were for just a trickle but now you're paying the full price." The beer. Well, there were those extra crates the driver "accidentally" forgot to charge for! Suddenly his memory came-back! I hadn't been paying the "propina" (tip-bribe-commission?) So that's how the bar was making a profit! How could I compete with the neighboring bars when they were all trickling and receiving deliveries from absent-minded drivers? There was only one way. Rent-out-the bar at weekends to "Beto Productions". They would advertise fiestas over the radio and in the colleges and campuses. Our rental fee guaranteed, they would be left with all the headaches.

It was late evening. Beto Productions had rented the entire bar. I rushed-over to check on the work. Speakers had been set-up outside, in-front of the bar. Loud music blasted-out across the Boulevard. Scantily dressed ladies danced suggestively on a small stage, but there were suspicious-looking curtains draped in front. Through the gap could be seen bright flashes from a disco-ball or strobe light. I thought about those Bourbon Street Bars back in New Orleans. You know the ones I mean. Yes, those! I began to wonder what was really going-on in my bar. Were they really dancing? Guys were lining-up round the block for entry. But where were the women? Finally a few young women entered. But what kind of women were they? I decided it was time to investigate. But wait, they wanted me to pay! "But it's my bar," I protested in my primitive Spanish as they called for the "Bouncer". Lucky break. Ricardo the bouncer spoke English. 'No problem Barry" he said, shouting above the vibrations of "Soul Freaks" & "Whose ya Daddy". "I'm a friend of Gene." A friend of Gene? Now I was really in trouble! Ricardo whispered loudly in my ear. "I supply his weed!" Supply his weed? "A pot-smoking FBI agent?"

There was a knock at my door. It was Soyla my bar manager. There was an emergency. Someone had stolen the bar DVD player. The "Punto de Encuentro" was the only bar on the Amazon Boulevard with a DVD player and giant TV screen. Without it we were naked. Customers came to drink and watch Latin music-videos of their favorite bands. It was a Video-Pub.

We rushed into town to buy a new DVD player. In the meantime "Rosa", my beautiful waitress, put the finger on someone. Oscar, a semi-regular customer, who went by the street name Mala Suerte (bad luck). Rosa reported him to the police. She had seen him leaving with a suspicious bulge in his pants. What was so unusual about that I wondered? Not such a rare sight in my bar or especially inside "Beta Productions" on a Saturday night. Good thing she hadn't seen me in front of those dancing girls I thought! Police searched Oscar's home but could find nothing. Just a few DVDs scattered across his bed in a house without electricity! Case closed - Not Guilty! And to think we had to pay them for the investigation.

Then there was that day. There he was. Gene (FBI), sitting at the bar. My Bar! Would I care for a drink? He was paying. Gene paying? Something was up that's for sure. He wanted to know if I would be going to his wedding! "Yes, Gene, count me in, who's the lucky lady?" "Rosa". "Congratulations Gene, I hope she's as nice as my waitress." "Yes, Rosa. I'm marrying your waitress!" "My waitress, Rosa?" "Yes we're in Love; I've even bought a ring!" How, I thought, could that beautiful young woman fall for this scam artist. It had to be the

"Badge!" I can't wait to go-back to "Toys are Us!"

Gene held his wedding reception (drinking fiesta) in a run-down apartment rented by his best friend Lenny. The whole family was present. They were ecstatic. Their beautiful young daughter Rosa was marrying an American with money (and a badge!). Maybe he would take her back with him to the States. Dancing and drinking until dawn with her sisters I noticed Lenny sitting in the shadows. "Lenny, I've lost my best waitress, and you; well you're losing a good friend to a beautiful young woman." "This could change Gene's life. Rosa could make a new man out of him." Lenny looked perplexed. "What's Gene going to do when we go-back to the States?" "He's going to be dead-meat, when his wife finds-out about this!" "About the wedding?" "Yes, the wedding - and her missing ring!"

Midnight Planting

Barry Seymour Brett

Victor, Michael (La Gallina) and Oscar Mala Suerte's brother, Carlos at the Midnight Planting

Surrounded by Rainforest, Iquitos sits on the Amazon, the most awesome river in the world. My house was finished. Now I was a proud homeowner in the jungle city but something was missing. What kind of jungle house would it be without a tree? Ernesto's son-in-law, Jose, built a quadrangle embellished with blue and white tiles. I checked with friends. Yes, they sold trees in the local markets. Visiting the Mercado Central I soon realized that they sold only young trees. They were too small and would take years to grow to maturity. Oscar (Mala Suerte-Bad Luck) and his younger brother Carlos knew of landscaping farms the other side of San Juan. We would go check-them-out. First we sped over to Victor's house to pick-up a shovel. Victor, afraid that Mala Suerte might steal his shovel, insisted on accompanying us.

As we drove through San Juan I thought back to the annual fiesta in honor of John the Baptist, the patron Saint of the City. In particular I recalled the fun and excitement of the "handkerchief dance". Twenty or thirty minutes the other side of San Juan we stopped at a landscaping farm, but no, they didn't have full-grown trees - just baby trees, the exact same trees I had seen at Mercado Central. Two more landscape places and still no luck. Riding with Mala Suerte was not helping!

Stopping at a roadside stand for sodas, a man working for the municipality told us of a likely source several miles further-out. Arriving at the locale I could see instantly that this was the oasis we had been searching for. There were hundreds of trees. The most magnificent and beautiful jungle trees imaginable. So many, and so varied. Victor and Mala Suerte wandered around with the shovel looking for the best ones, but unfortunately many of the best looking trees were not suitable for growing in street locations. They required a jungle setting to prosper. Those capable of surviving in an urban setting were not so attractive. The owner of the plot was in Lima, a thousand miles away. Without her permission we couldn't take one. Feeling a little despondent we left in a motokaro.

On the way back we passed a church in the suburbs of San Juan. There were several nice looking trees lining the front. "Oscar, that's the kind of tree I want, about that size, not fully-grown. I know they survive in an urban setting, there's one just like it down my street". "Barry that's a Fica Tree, they thrive well and don't require a lot of maintenance." "We could shape-it into a monkey or parrot, that way it won't grow too big." "My uncle's got a Fica tree in his backyard."

It was a warm Amazon night. Someone was tapping at my window. Climbing out of bed I glanced at the clock. Gone one o'clock! It was Victor carrying his shovel. "Barry open the door, Michael and Carlos are carrying the tree, we need a flash light and a bowl of water." "What tree?" "You know, Oscar's Uncle, that tree". "But it's one o'clock in the morning" "I know Barry, we had to wait for Oscar's Uncle to fall asleep. His Aunt wanted to sell it!" "She needed money for a new dress." "Where's Miguel and Mala Suerte?" "Oh, they took-off in Miguel's motokaro to find some Guano. We need guano to nourish the tree. It's suffering from shock right now, we have to nurse it back to health!" Suddenly there was a loud roar as Miguel's motokaro, the one with the cracked-exhaust tube, turned the corner and came to a halt in front of the tree. "We found some guano in the cemetery!" "The cemetery! At two in the morning? Didn't it give you the creeps?" "Not really, at least we weren't chased by a dog." "A dog, wait a minute, your pants are ripped, that's a dog bite!" "Barry, he chased us with a dog and a flashlight. I need medical attention!" "Who, who chased you?" "Oscar's Uncle? "The Church Watchman in San Juan!" "The Church! Oh boy, I need to go pray" "But Mala Suerte told me his Uncle had a Fica Tree in the backyard. I gave him $50 for his Aunt's new dress." "Mala Suerte's Uncle lives in a stilt house above the river. They have no backyard!"

Rone would drop-bye once a week to take care of my Fica Tree. Oscar and Miguel took-off to the cemetery in a motokaro to get more Guano. I later discovered that "Guano" is really accumulated bird-droppings that at one-time covered a large part of several Peruvian islands. A huge export business developed. Until it was finally exhausted, Peruvian Guano was the best fertilizer in the world! Nowadays, locals refer to any good-quality soil as Guano.

"Rone whatever's wrong with my tree. I paid the kids $50 for it. I've only had it a few weeks and already it's wilting and the leaves are turning brown. I thought it was an evergreen. They don't have "Fall" down here do they?" "Barry, it's dying, soon it'll be dead. They chopped the roots-off too close to the trunk. Maybe they were in a hurry to get away! Woof-woof!"

Carrying my baby tree from the Mercado Central I passed a beautiful full-grown Fica. For a moment it reminded me of those church trees in San Juan. I wondered which of the trees was missing, and if it had it been replaced. My new tree is nothing like the "Church Tree", way smaller, but at least it was acquired honestly and probably with time it will grow. One day maybe people will sit beneath its shade, but for now the cats love it and the dogs salute it with their hind leg!

Victor and Oscar (Mala Suerte) Examining the Trees and Foliage

The Midnight Tree

AMAZON Frontier Town

Barry Seymour Brett

Leticia, on the River Amazon, sits at the junction of three countries. Columbia, Peru and Brazil. The quiet peaceful cultures of the Amazon Rainforest clash with the flamboyant lifestyles of the Western Brazilians and the darker side of the Columbian Drug Cartels. It's a **"free zone city."** People from each of the three countries are free to live, move around and work in any area without passports or other documents. The local people are very proud of that fact. They've got to be kidding! People from all over the world (and distant planets) are free to move around and work anywhere in the U.S. without documents! Plus in the U.S. they can get all kinds of benefits for free backed-by worthless bonds sold to foreign governments. Schooling and dental assistance for their kids, medical aid for pregnant immigrants and free coffee at "Starbucks" on Sundays. In California, Martians can get their horns cleaned and filled at State expense!

At the Amazon Frontier the countries are so close together that some buildings straddle across Columbia into Brazil. Drinking Columbian coffee on the front porch with friends, I felt the need to leave. The backyard toilet was nothing more than a hole in the ground. There was a narrow ditch in front breached by a wooden plank. Two sheets of corrugated iron shielded the toilet from view. Upon returning my friend enquired "How did you like Brazil, Barry?" "Come-on now, I only used the restroom." "Well, our house is in Columbia but the toilet is on the other side of the ditch, in Brazil!" So that's why it's a **"free zone city**." "Your passport sir?" "But I'm in a hurry" "Your visa's expired, you need to apply for an extension" "I can't wait! - I've got to go **now!**" "Sorry sir, renewals take six to eight weeks" "Can't you issue a transit visa?" "I'm only going to the back of the yard!" "You should have applied sooner!" "But I'm desperate". "Don't worry sir; they sell corks in the pharmacy across the street - in Peru!"

Bars and discotheques lined the main drag. Renzo and his brother Carlos carried pistols. Some pedestrians displayed their weapons in full view. Renzo reminded me that it was **"just for show!"** "The ladies like a big gun!" "Well maybe so, but don't you need a license?" "Barry, my license is my **finger on the trigger!"** As we entered the "El Dorado", Renzo and Carlos checked their weapons-in. Padlocked "Gun Security Lockers" were available at the entrance. There was a large padlocked trunk to the side for Machetes, Rifles and Shotguns! Riddled with bullet holes, a sign in Spanish above the bar read "Fist fights only". This would put "Dodge City" to shame I thought as three beautiful young ladies sat on our laps.

Toward the center of the barroom was a long pole ascending upwards through a hole in the ceiling. It brought back memories of that drunken birthday party for the Fire chief in Rockville Maryland, back in the seventies. But this was no civilized firemen's bash. This was the "Amazon Frontier" and there it was, directly in front of us "The Sliding Pole!" Young ladies slid down the pole as young men slid-up! Out front was a row of gambling tables. Young ladies (and young men) stood to the side vying for attention. Players gambled for "Keys to a room!" All the time loud Spanish Rock Music bellowed-out from speakers, drowning-out the curses and threats as the players became angry and violent. It was time to leave.

Hailing a cab, Renzo filled-me-in. Cab drivers were not to be trusted. Passengers could find themselves robbed or even raped. Not to worry, I thought. Renzo has his **finger on the trigger!** Better remember to send that donation to the National Rifle Association when I get-back to the States! At the riverside, small boats ferried passengers across to Santa Rosa, the Peruvian immigration check-point. On a small island, Carlos described Santa Rosa as boring and derelict. They would not be able to enter armed. At least, not without paying a bribe! With plenty of time to kill, we settled for a boat ride to a riverside restaurant. Renzo described it as romantic and affordable. Renzonian translation. There would be good-looking hookers at a reasonable price! Surprise, surprise. The food was excellent and much to the disappointment of Renzo, no young ladies of the night were anywhere to be found.

Nearby was a Street Fiesta. A Columbian band played romantic "Vallenato's." Columbian music is famous throughout the Amazon region. Blended with Brazilian influences it forms the basis of "Cumbia", by far the most popular dance music of the region. Dancing here in Leticia was very formal compared to the jungle cities of the interior. In Iquitos and Yurimaguas boys would dance in groups with other boys, their brothers, cousins or neighborhood friends. The very young danced with the very old. Young women danced with their sisters or obviously much older men. Parents and Grandparents would dance with their children and grandchildren.

The abundant jungle atmosphere of love and compassion toward friends and relatives was not present here. Revelers were not dancing in groups, only strictly in pairs. Girls were not dancing with girls and boys did not dance with boys. This Street Fiesta had more in common with dances in Northern Europe or the U.S. Ice cold indifference, sticking with one partner, afraid to mingle, embarrassed to be seen dancing (especially with Mum or Dad or someone much older or younger or someone of the same sex). It brought back memories of "Oktoberfest", Munich, Germany. The ultimate cold party. All the inhibitions, the European and North American fear of enjoying one's self, of having a good time were present there. Munich Beer-Fest. "Its fun, I like it, but it's wrong. We shouldn't be doing this, but it's OK as long as we're drunk!"

Before returning to Peru I wanted to buy some boxes of Columbian chocolate. The Amazonian People describe Columbian chocolate as the best in the world. I wasn't sure I could trust their judgment. After all, their ancestors grew-up on rubber plantations. That's why their omelets are stodgy and bounce off the floor like a rubber ball! Pizzas are smothered with strands of cheese that snap-back into the dough like elastic bands. Biting into a hotdog, I was reminded of a bicycle inner tube! I wondered what kind of chocolate it would be. Sugar-coated rubber sprinkled with chocolate and Brazilian nuts?

I soon realized that the **"free zone"** didn't apply to me. Arriving at the Peruvian check-point I was denied entry without a Brazilian exit stamp. A five minute boat ride and we were back in Brazil. The Brazilians wanted proof that I had entered from Columbia! What kind of proof did they want? A **"toilet roll!"** - A **"cork!"**

Copyright October 2009

Jungle Walk

Barry Seymour Brett

Waiting for it's Prey

Sitting in the Plaza de Armas early one morning I noticed my neighbor's son Oscar cleaning shoes. He was soon joined by his older brother, Carlos. "We're trying to scrape-up some money to go visit my Aunt" he said, "She's expecting a baby any-day now." I reached into my pocket for some small change to pay for a mototaxi. "No, no Barry, we can't get there by taxi. Let's walk. It's a nice day."

Starting-out early in the morning we walked for an hour or so through the city streets. We passed the school where Carlos studied until the money ran-out. Soon we were outside the City and walking through jungle growth. We crossed the Nanay river in a small boat, walked past a few villages until the trees and foliage were thick and difficult to pass. Trails led thru to a small clearing. Carlos swung his machete from side-to-side to clear a path. His brother swung his - wait a minute that's not a machete! No public restrooms in the jungle!

We reached the clearing. I sensed imminent danger. There it was, directly in front of us. Beckoning us - daring us to approach. Every hiker's worse nightmare. Snakebite, anybody? No. "The rope-walk."

- 65 -

You know the one I mean. Swaying from side-to-side. The one with those missing planks! I was afraid to look-down. It didn't matter anyway. I couldn't see the bottom without my eyeglasses. Reaching for my eyeglasses I missed-my-step. My legs straddling the missing planks, I struggled to hold-on to the rope handles. I could see birds perched on the far-side of the ropeway. Vultures maybe? I glanced upward to see if they were circling above, waiting for their chance. As I put-on my glasses, I looked thru the gap in the planks only to realize I needed a telescope! The chasm resembled a bottomless pit. I tried to think of something positive, like "Tarzan", "Indy Jones" or a "Parachute!" Carlos grabbed me by the arm and plank-by-plank led me to safety! Standing on safe-ground and wearing my glasses I could see the vultures were nothing more than two brightly colored Macaws. I looked-back across the chasm toward the rope-walkway. Two young boys crossed. They pranced around, laughing and joking as they skipped-over the missing planks, buckets of water balanced on their shoulders!

It was approaching midday and we were getting hungry. Carlos climbed a tree, cutting-down a huge ants' nest. Thousands of ants scrambled from the mound as it crashed to the ground. Grabbing a few clumps of ants, Carlos placed them in plastic bags. Dinnertime! I tried to imagine what they might taste like. Fried with Yucca, in an omelet, or maybe stuck in peanut butter with a splattering of strawberry jelly! I remembered those horrible chocolate-coated ants in Paris, France. With hindsight they didn't seem so bad! Plastic bags squirming with ants strapped to their belts, Carlos and his brother walked a half mile or so looking for a house where we might rest and hopefully cook. There it was on the banks of a stream. A wooden shack. An elderly man beckoned us inside and soon Carlos and his brother were preparing lunch. Yes, it was a fry-up, together with Yucca and Platanos (bananas). I tasted a bunch of fried ants. Yes, I could see how *some-people* might get addicted to them. Maybe the fried ants could be marketed in a bottle and sold at Walmart's Pharmacy, on the same shelf as the other laxatives!

We sat-around and talked for a while, then suddenly I had the urge to leave. It was an urgent urge! I raced-over to the hole-in-the-ground, making sure there were no live ants lingering around, waiting their chance to get revenge! Feeling relieved, I returned to the shack to find Carlos standing next to a small boat and carrying a fishing pole. "But there's Crocs out there and I can't swim," I shouted in Spanglish as we pushed the boat into the creek. Les than five minutes into the trip and there they were. Their dinosauric eyes staring at us as they contemplated a tasty meal. Rocking the boat, Carlos made several brave attempts to navigate the boat around the Crocs. We drifted down river several miles until we reached a small shore-side community. Carlos and Oscar knew exactly where they were, their cousins lived close-by.

After a brief trek down a jungle trail we arrived at the Aunt's house. She burst into tears as we approached the door. There were hugs and more tears. Carlos is 19, his brother 17. They were 14 and 12 last time they saw their Aunt. It was a baby boy! They talked for long time, played soccer outside with some neighborhood kids and then we drank a couple of sodas as the Aunt prepared Lunch. It was fish with Platano and Heart-of-the-Palm. Whilst waiting for lunch the Uncle showed me the gaping hole in the roof. Good thing it wasn't raining. The wind had blown half the roof away during the night. They needed to patch-it-up with leaves from the surrounding trees. After lunch, without the benefit of electricity, radio or television, the family entertained each other by singing and playing zamponya. No electronic games or other distractions. Just a simple pack of cards rounded-off the day's events.

Afterwards we walked-back down the jungle trail toward the shoreline. On the way we stopped at a small lagoon to look for giant turtles. Near the shore was a run-down bar, next to a discotheque. Visitors seldom came. This was a big village event as we strolled along the shore. We were a huge hit, as eligible young women in the village rushed-over to the discotheque to meet us. Parading in front of us, the young girls were escorted by their mother or an older sister. But the mothers and older sisters wanted all the action! They pushed and shoved each other to gain an audience. The better-looking ones were trampled in the rush. "It fits My Lord!" "No it doesn't, it fits me!!!" We couldn't stick-around for the clock to strike midnight, we needed to get-away fast. I looked for the Pumpkin Coach but it was missing!

The journey home was difficult. It was getting dark and the mosquitoes seemed to bite harder and more-often than before. With just a flashlight to guide us we wound our way along the croc infested river. Avoiding the rope-walk, we crossed a rickety old bridge. Carlos caught a small fish which he placed in a bag and strapped it around his waste. Finally we arrived back in the City. We went-over to Carlos's house and he and his younger brother told the good news about the baby boy as they handed Mum the fish. They talked for a while about the trip to his Aunt's house. As I left I couldn't help but think how different life is here in the Amazon jungle. People are alive! If this had been California, Carlos's Mum would just have picked-up the phone. "Hi, how you doing?" "It's a baby boy!" "Congratulations Honey, say hi to the Dad!" End of a cold, pitiful electronic conversation. No hugs, No tears of joy, No jungle walks, No rope-walks, No crocs to liven-up the trip, No sing-songs with zamponya, No Cinderella-Moment and no exercise! Just a simple two-minute phone-call. But wait a moment, did I say no ANTS? Sign me-up, I think I need a cell-phone!

Brazilian Pirate

Barry Seymour Brett

There were several large boats at the dockside plying for passengers. Very few Brazilians speak Spanish or English. I didn't really understand what they were saying, but I'm sure they knew I wanted a passage to Yurimaguas, a large city on the banks of the River Amazon. A five day trip down-river, most passengers sleep below deck in hammocks, but I wanted my own private cabin. I chose the "Lust". Ronaldo, the captain's mate spoke English and Spanish and the Captain, Veronica, spoke Portuguese with only a smattering of Spanish. She was a beautiful young woman in her late twenties. Not into fashion, she wore a pair of cut-offs and a captain's hat with gold braid and an anchor. Marcos, one of the crew members carried my bags onto the "Lust" and placed them in my cabin.

The following afternoon Ronaldo sat-down in my cabin and told me about Veronica's childhood. Her father and brother were seamen. The loan survivor of a Brazilian family of four, Veronica inherited her father's boat, the "Lust". River people had known Veronica since she was a child, plying the river alongside her dad. "She's got a nasty temper. Just like her dad". "She's a sweet lady but she trades with smugglers and drug barons and has been known to hide contraband beneath her bra and even inside her private part!"

Later that evening I wandered below deck. Dodging in-between the hammocks, I finally reached the galley. Roberta, the beautiful Brazilian cook, was preparing a plate of rice with Brazilian sausage. There was little else to choose from. Not speaking Portuguese, I pointed to a plate of fried chicken and rice. In the meantime Ronaldo arrived looking for a cold beer. Several minutes passed before Roberta plunked down the plate of chicken and "What!" "Ronaldo can you help me? I wanted chicken with rice, not with fried snails!" As I took a bite Ronaldo explained. "Barry they don't serve chicken. This is fried majas with Amazonian grubs!" "But Ronaldo it looks and tastes a bit like chicken, what kind of bird are these majas? "They're not birds, they're rodents." "Are you kidding me, you mean rats! Don't they spread bubonic plague?" "Don't worry; they're fruit eating rodents". "What are you saying Ronaldo? If I feed a rat bananas and oranges he's going to taste good!"

The following morning we pulled into a small port and took-on bananas and some additional passengers. Ronaldo, wanting to practice his English, joined me for a while. As we were talking the boat's engines cut. A short while later and the river police boarded to check our papers. "We might have to pay-off the river police." "Are we smuggling?" "Barry, you can't make money carrying passengers!" "But, the police; they've gone below deck" "They're not checking for drugs or contraband, the problem is Roberta." "Roberta the cook?" "Her passport describes her as a man but now she's a woman. "Roberta is really a man!" "But those hips and everything?" "Those Brazilian surgeons in Rio are real good. Barry she was a man before but now she's every bit a woman." "Really, **every bit**?" Ronaldo, this surgeon in Rio, how much does he charge? Does he perform "enlargements" on **every bit**?" "A stroke of luck. The Police Chief has been making-eyes at Veronica!" "Gosh, I hope **she** hasn't had an "identity change!" An hour later and the Chief left to re-board the police-launch alongside. As he climbed down the side of the "Lust" he waved at Veronica and gave a broad smile.

That evening I went below deck. This would be the final night aboard the "Lust". There was a warm Amazon breeze blowing through the lower deck as I approached the galley. At the edge of the food-bar and across from Roberta the cook sat a pet monkey chained to a table. A man played Columbian Ballads on an accordion and everyone was dancing. It was hot and humid below deck with very little space. Drinking Tarapoto wine and Trago (sex in the jungle), young girls and guys, grandma and pops all danced wildly between the oil drums and piles of bananas.

As I joined in the wild dancing I thought about my California neighbors. Leaving for a Caribbean Cruise, two sets of golf clubs and six or seven giant suitcases lined the sidewalk as they waited for the limo to take them to the airport. Visiting them the night before, I watched as they packed away tuxedos, nightgowns and robes. One case alone contained all they would need to open-up a local beauty parlor! Another case looked like a miniature pharmacy. Once aboard the Cruise Ship, they would dance in an air-conditioned ballroom where everyone spoke English. Dressed to kill in full attire, they would listen to corny jokes from the Master of Ceremonies whilst reminiscing about days long since gone! Wining and dining on exotic foods prepared by a world class chef they would go away thinking what great value it was for the few thousand dollars they had loaded onto the card! But, with a captain wearing cut-offs, a cook serving fruit-eating rodents who used to be a man but was now **every bit** a woman, who on earth needs a beauty parlor in a suitcase? I'll take the monkey, Brazilian sausages and oil drums any day I thought, as a beautiful young lady accompanied me back to my cabin!!

It was early morning on the final day. The cook brought me a bowl of broth with Brazilian sausages. Bare-bones meals were included in the cabin fare. Coffee was extra! As I glanced out the cabin window I could see a cargo vessel pulling alongside. Sipping on my coffee, I could hear a general commotion amongst the crew as passengers who could understand Portuguese fled the upper deck to hide below! But, Veronica; where was her hat with the gold braid? Now she was wearing a red headscarf and her make-up; it was all smudged – or was it? Ronaldo filled-me-in. "We are going to rendezvous with smugglers. Veronica thinks she's a pirate! That red lipstick streaked across her face and under her eyes strikes fear in her enemies. She's been known to draw blood" Sounded like my nurse at the chemotherapy sessions, I thought! But a pirate? I thought only men were pirates. Woman's lib on the banks of the Amazon!

As we pulled alongside the cargo vessel, Veronica shouted-out at the captain and crew. Reminiscent of a traffic back-up on the Golden State Freeway, there was shouting, hand gestures and unseemly Spanish vulgarities. Then out-came the guns and knives! Ronaldo explained. "We've reached the rendezvous point. Veronica has an axe to grind with the captain. He's her ex-lover and he owes her ten barrels of oil. We're going to board their ship." "Board another vessel? But I only paid to sail in this one. Can I get a refund, I want to get-off!" "Are you with us, or against us?" "Is there no middle ground?" "That's plank talk! Barry, you don't want to mess with Veronica when she's mad."

"Look, I'm a foreigner. I could be in a lot of trouble, boarding a vessel for plunder." "We're not going to seize any oil drums. We're going aboard to negotiate." "Negotiate? With guns and knives!" "They're smugglers we need to protect ourselves." "Don't worry Barry; if we have to, Veronica knows people who can alter your identity with false papers." "Oh yes, you mean like Roberta the cook!"

Suddenly the shouting ceased, the crew put away their weapons and the Captain of the cargo boat climbed aboard. Handing over a bottle of Jamaican Rum, the Captain hugged Veronica. "But Ronaldo, I thought we were boarding them!" "It's settled Barry. Drums of oil for Russian vodka, Cuban cigars and a crate of fake Rolex watches made in China. For a brief moment I was really disappointed. My adrenalin rush had come to a sudden end. Unfulfilled, I really felt like boarding the vessel! What was wrong with me I wondered? All the other passengers were hiding below and yet there I was, standing on deck disappointed because the adventure had been cancelled! Veronica the Pirate had sold us-out for some watches and Cuban cigars! It took almost an hour to un-load the drums and lift the crate on board, but soon we were back on-course for Yurimaguas. As we prepared to dock at Yurimaguas, Veronica washed-off her war-paint and changed into a sexy outfit. Young men at the dockside wolf-whistled as Veronica walked down the gangplank, wiggling her hips as she carried her bottle of Jamaican Rum. Ronaldo and Marcos together with other crew members unloaded the oil drums, bananas and the crate of cigars, vodka and Rolex watches.

Booking-into a small hotel across from the main Plaza, I could see Veronica and Marcos sitting in the square in the evening swigging on the booze. They were soon joined by a couple of girl friends and an older man. This strong daunting young woman who just hours before had stood bestride the deck of the "Lust", negotiating with brigands and smugglers, was now just one of many young ladies, hanging-out in the Plaza de Armas. Just as I had struggled to understand her Portuguese, now she would struggle to understand their Spanish. The magic of piracy was fading fast and soon would be nothing more than a distant memory. It was getting late, almost time for bed. As I walked away from the hotel balcony, I rolled a Cuban Cigar, took a sip of Russian Vodka and checked the time on my Rolex. Would I risk sailing with Veronica the Pirate again I wondered? You bet your life I would!

Chocolatada

Barry Seymour Brett

Pouring-out the Hot Chocolate at the Chocolatada for Street Orphans

It was approaching Christmas. I was looking forward to helping those less fortunate than myself (most of the city). With limited funds, I wondered how that could be done in an isolated jungle city of half a million souls. It would be an impossible task. Neglected by the central government in Lima, Iquitos suffers from enormous poverty. Ernesto, the Master-Builder, who had helped to construct my house, came-up with a plan. We would promote a fund-raiser out-front his house and the proceeds were to go toward "The Chocolatada for Street Orphans."

The fund-raiser was a "parrillada" (BBQ). Tickets are pre-sold. The proceeds pay for the cost of the food and the excess is used for the specified purpose. Most the money is made from the sale of beer and sodas which are never included in the ticket price. I had bought tickets for ten of my friends. It didn't take long to realize that there were not many people present at the "BBQ'. Ten, to be exact! "But Ernesto, you haven't sold one ticket." "It's Christmas Barry, my friends have no money." "Don't worry, Barry" "We'll make money off the beer" he said, as I paid for another round! "Good thing the soccer players showed-up, we'll make a mountain of money once the game starts." The game commenced.

"We've brought-in the best soccer players in the community," Ernesto's son explained. Other teams know they'll probably lose tonight but it's an opportunity to play against the best while supporting a good cause. Suddenly there was no space left at the BBQ tables. It seemed like the entire neighborhood wanted a piece of the action. Ernesto's wife rushed-off to buy more hot dogs and buns to feed the growing multitude. It was gone midnight and still the games continued! Loud music bellowed-out from a couple of speakers as spectators chugged down the beer and stuffed their faces with hot dogs, hamburgers and churros.

A few days before the 'Chocolatada', Ernesto's wife showed-up at my front door. "We're going-out to buy the toys" she said, dragging me into a mototaxi. We parked in-front of a toy store. Inside were bins of discounted toys. Hundreds of tiny plastic cars, spinning tops, balls and dolls. We sifted through the bins picking-out the more desirable toys. But wait a minute. That wasn't permitted - mix and match! They were having none of it. Suddenly the price doubled! We needed 300 toys. I reached into my pocket but I didn't have enough with me! I turned to Ernesto's wife. No, Ernesto didn't give her enough money. She didn't expect to pay so much, but she could get money from the fundraiser in the morning. What good is that I thought? We needed to buy the toys that day. I rushed-over to the ATM.

The central feature of Christmas Dinner and the "Chocolatada" is the "Paneton". A rich, distinctive tasting cake, packed with fruit. Originating in Italy, "Paneton" swept through Peru during the "Rubber Boom" of the 1800s to become the "star" of the Christmas table. Christmas without "Paneton" is like a "Pub with no Beer". Visiting local markets, I noticed that there were various brands, mostly produced in Peru. The better cakes were sealed in large metal cans, decorated with Papa Noel (Santa Clause), Holley and Golden Bells. "Todino Paneton", imported from Italy was generally considered the best.How many "Panetons" would we need for 300 kids? Probably forty.

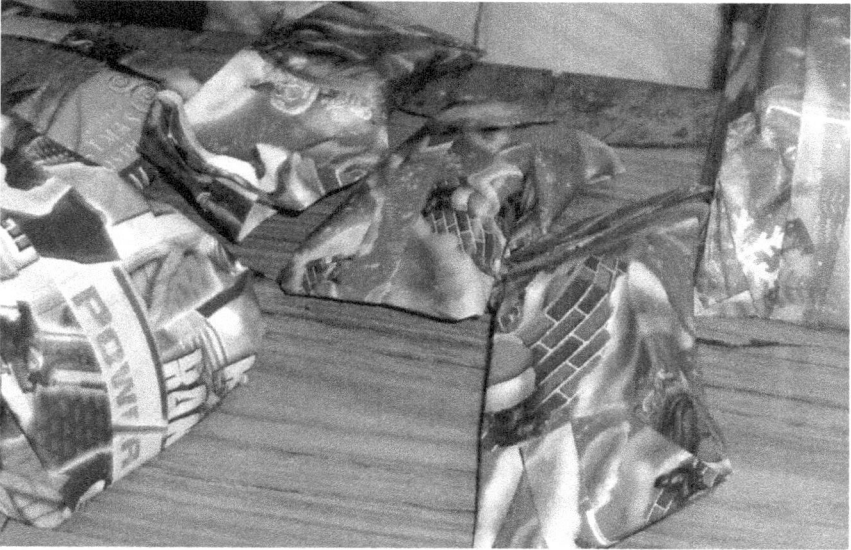
Wrapped Toys for the Christmas Chocolatada

Clown handing-out toys and hot chocolate at the Christmas Chocolatada

We scoured around looking for a deal. There they were, piled sky-high on a makeshift table in the Belen Market. What a stroke of luck, and so cheap. Well, they wouldn't be the top-brand Italian imports at that price. Surprise, surprise. They were imported from China! Walmart would love to get their greedy hands on these I thought, as I opened-one-up looking for noodles and a fortune cookie!

Christmas Day. Ernesto and his wife were exhausted. They had spent the best part of two days wrapping presents, preparing the food and setting-up tables. Everything was set-up in front of Ernesto's house. Two huge barrels of chocolate drink were bubbling on the stove as children started to arrive. Ernesto's wife ladled the hot chocolate into cups. Every child got a cup of hot chocolate, slice of paneton and a toy. We hired a clown to entertain the kids and hand-out the toys and every toy was attractively wrapped and marked, boy or girl. Some kids were greedier than others! Familiar faces kept appearing in the toy line as a stereo in the courtyard blasted-out Christmas songs. Those wonderful jungle kids began to dance like there was no tomorrow.

I went away satisfied that all those impoverished kids will remember Christmas day at the Chocolatada for the rest of their lives. Most of them had no shoes. Almost all of them had never owned a toy. I plan on organizing another fund-raiser next Christmas. In the meantime I shall be renting a clown outfit - I have to replenish my bank account somehow!

The Sound of Music

Barry Seymour Brett

Music is the life force of the Amazon Jungle Cities. Nowhere in the world will you find a people more heavily influenced by music and dance than here in Iquitos. Surrounded by thousands of miles of rainforest, Iquitos stands at the junction of Brazil and Columbia. Musical influences flow down from the hills around Cuzco and trickle across the border with Bolivia. There are additional musical contributions from the various native tribes that inhabit the surrounding rainforest. The music of preference is Cumbia. A blend of Columbian, Brazilian and Peruvian music. Large dance bands such as "Explosion", "Papillon" and "Los Carabenos" perform Cumbia in local venues complete with dancing girls. And do the girls know how to dance? You better believe they do!

It was early evening. I was heading over to my friend Jack's house. Jack was a motor-bike enthusiast, a "Biker". Motorbikes are the main form of transportation here in Iquitos. Biking was his life. Jack was in heaven! As I approached his house I could hear the sound of music. A loud band was playing Cumbia on a makeshift stage as jungle girls wiggled and twisted their bodies to the beat. The street had been closed-off and giant speakers had been erected at each end. Dozens of improvised stands sold cheap vino (wine) and "Climax" (alcoholic carbonated soda). There were BBQ stands and burger-stands. Hundreds of residents were dancing and drinking in the street. It was a "Street Fiesta!"

Men, women, children, teenagers, grandma and pops. Everyone was singing, drinking and dancing. Everyone except Jack! There he was, standing outside his front door looking miserable and upset. "What's up Jack?" "This Street Fiesta. It's driving me crazy. I can't concentrate on my reading!" he shouted as he sipped on a Pisco-Sour (brandy-grape liqueur). "Reading?" What on Earth can he be reading that's so important that he can't get-out and dance, I wondered. "Jack, music is "La Energia de la Selva" (The Energy of the Jungle)" "Look at all these people, having a good time. Dance and music. It's everything to them; they are your neighbors Jack." "Let's go out and dance." "Barry, I want it shut down!" he screamed, trying to be heard above the music as he sipped on another Pisco Sour. "But Jack, you're the one who's always spouting about individual freedom. How we've lost it all in the U.S. How wonderful it feels to chug-down a six-pack while riding a bike without a helmet or license - and as fast as you like! "Barry I want it shut-down!" "I've called the police; they'll be here any minute now."

Two hours later the police arrived. Yes, they could try to shut it down, but it would cost $100! Well that's the end of that I thought, as Jack reached into his pocket and coughed-up the money! "You've got to be kidding Jack, $100! That's a big piece of money round these parts." "It's 11 and I'm tired. I need to rest." The cops left with the money.

Midnight and the street party was rocking and rolling. The music got louder as more neighbors arrived from adjacent streets to join-in the dancing. Some neighbors were sitting on Jack's wall, while others threw empty beer bottles and trash in his driveway. Jack was agitated. There they were, driving down the street toward Jack's house. The cops on their motor-bikes. But wait, they were swinging around a bottle of rum and they had passengers on the back now! "They spent my money on hookers and rum" Jack screamed, as the cops parked their bikes in his driveway, escorting their lady-friends and joining in the dancing! "I'll call the Chief, that'll put a stop to it". "Jack, why don't you just hang-it-up for the night." I really didn't want to get involved. I felt this was Jack's problem. Besides, if he shut the party down maybe they would form a lynch party and come looking for us!

It was almost one o'clock in the morning when the Chief arrived. The bombshell hit. "Sir, we can't shut it down, it's their right. If they want a party then they can have one. It's not for us to trample on their rights; we're just police officers doing our job. You're an American. Surely you of all people must know that governments can't interfere with people's rights".

I had a sudden flash-back to that rowdy surfers' party in Huntington Beach, California. It kicked-off about nine at night. Neighbors called and complained. By ten the building was surrounded by squad cars and thirty or more police, some in riot gear. A helicopter hovered overhead, its laser-like searchlight illuminating the kegs and scantily dressed females. A Public Address System bellowed-out "Shut the party down now", waking-up half the city in the process. The property-owner was threatened with a stiff fine and a law-suit. Party-goers were hit with batons. Others were arrested.

Jack looked perplexed as he sipped on his Pisco Sour. "But officer, I have rights too, what about my rights?" "Yes sir you do. You can throw a wild party tomorrow night if you wish". Jack pleaded with him as he handed the Chief $50 for his troubles!" "But the noise, what about my right to live in peace in my own home." "Well sir that's entirely up to you. You put a roof on your house because you didn't want to get wet. If you wanted to live in silence you should have sound-proofed your home. They sell cheap ear-muffs in the pharmacy downtown." Jack's blood was beginning to boil. I rushed the Chief out the front door.

It was one-thirty in the morning. Jack was in no mood for conversation. "Sorry Jack but I have to leave now" I said as I moved toward the door. "But Barry I can give you a ride back to your place on my bike, if you like. " "An angry, "Pisco-sipping Biker" without a helmet and a license?" "No thanks Jack." "I'm going out-front to dance in the street and exercise my Peruvian (American???) Rights of freedom!"

Shroom Man

Barry Seymour Brett

Jeremiah with his Basket of Magic Mushrooms!

It was Thanksgiving Dinner at the Amazon Golf Course, Iquitos, Peru. Sitting across from me was Jeremiah the "Shroom Man." A small basket on the table held more than a dozen types of mushroom. Without the benefit of cranberry sauce we were about to savor the wonders of jungle mushroom sauce.

But the "Shroom Man." I saw him only a week ago selling mushrooms on the Amazon Boulevard to my friend Bill. That's strange; I haven't seen Bill lately, or his girl friend! Gosh, we're a long way from the hospital, out here in the rainforest. "How safe are they?" "Don't worry Barry; I've been harvesting mushrooms for ten years. Mostly in Oregon and Northern California. I know everything there is to know about them." "I fry them, cook them in pies, sauté them with mountain butter and herbs, even smoke them!" "Smoke them? How can you smoke mushrooms?" "I pound them to a powder and mix the mushroom with mapacho jungle tobacco. Then I wrap it in an hallucinogenic toe (tow-wey) leaf from the ayahuasca vine to give it an extra kick!" "I go mushrooming in the early hours of the morning. Deep in the rainforest on all fours, talking to them, singing to them, scouring the ground with a flashlight!" Oh really, was that before or after he smoked them I wondered! Talking to them! Singing to them! Maybe he even sang "with them". Alice did things like that after she ate the mushrooms. And Alice didn't smoke them! As we talked about smoking mushrooms my mind flashed-back to that rehab center in Whittier, California. Visiting a relative hooked on amphetamines and cocaine, and before I had a chance to enter the facility, a street bum approached my car. "You can always check yourself in afterwards" he said as he offered to sell me heroine and a syringe!

Mother warned me about mushrooms when I was a boy. Deadly Nightshade and Belladonna. I'm scared to death of them. I only eat mushrooms from a can. At least my relatives could sue the manufacturer for funeral expenses! But fresh mushrooms in the produce section. No way. Those immigrant farm workers have no sympathy for us Angloids! A smidgen of Belladonna here, a splattering of Deadly Nightshade there. Who would know who would care? They're not FDA approved either. How could they be? Mushrooms don't spend weeks or months growing in a field where they can be observed, monitored and checked for diseases and crop parasites. They can't even be checked for fungus, they are a fungus! They sprout-up overnight in a dung heap! Poor Barry, what a tragic ending, paralyzed from the waist down, in agony and vomiting. Belladonna juice oozing from his eyeballs

"Barry, this sauce is a combination of several different species. The mushrooms in the basket are just a sampling of those I used to prepare the sauce. Each mushroom retains certain characteristics. Hallucinogenic, therapeutic and anti-cancer properties. I didn't use the big ones. Those big ones are deadly poison. If you touch them you need go wash your hands in a hurry. The slightest amount and "Poof" you're gone! "Really, the slightest amount? My mother in-law likes mushrooms". "The small ones in the basket enhance sexual re-generation." "Oh yeah, you've got to be kidding me, sexual regeneration!! To hell with mother's advice, give me ten of the small ones!" "By the way, what exactly do you mean by enhanced sexual re-generation?" "I was only born with one. Will more sprout-out around my waist?" "Will they grow into different shapes and sizes? Or is it one size fits all?" "Is that what they mean by "Magic Mushrooms?"
There I was at the Amazon Golf Course on Thanksgiving Day

mingling with shipping magnates, oil tycoons and local newspaper editors. Young girls sat on their laps as they sipped jungle wine and ate turkey dinner laced with hallucinogenic mushroom sauce! I used to think Californians knew how to party! But this is the Jungle. Unlike California, no-one got bent out-of-shape. There was no undercover investigation. No arrests and no hair follicle analysis. Tranquil and peaceful, the energy of the jungle dissipates the mindless, relentless pursuit of uniformity emanating from up North. It was Thanksgiving Day and so an "EXTRA" prayer before dinner was definitely in order. The "Mushroom Prayer." I only hope He's listening, I thought. But what happens I wondered, when I take unnecessary risk, fully aware of the possible consequences? Am I still covered? Or maybe there's an exclusion for reckless behavior. Surely he doesn't cover everything, does He? I was a little hesitant when the mushroom sauce arrived. I'm not exactly a mushroom tasting connoisseur; it's a dangerous profession to be in. It didn't really taste like mushrooms, at least not like the ones I'd eaten before. But then I'd never tasted Belladonna!

Thanksgiving had come and gone and Christmas Day had almost arrived. There was a knock at my door. It was my good friend Paul, the Amazon shipping magnate. "Barry they've got a Christmas Dinner at the Amazon Golf Course. Are you going?" "Who's going to be there?" "Barry, there's going to be dancing, plenty of beautiful young women and Jeremiah the "Shroom-Man" will be preparing the soup and cooking pumpkin pies". I walked over to the bedroom and checked in the wall-mirror. Almost a month had gone-bye and yet nothing was sprouting-out! Feeling a little despondent I returned to the living room. "Well, Barry, are you going?" "Paul, I need to think about it. The soup and the pies; do they come with a guarantee?

Baby in a Box

Barry Seymour Brett

Baby in a Box in front of the Casa de Fierro; the Iron House.

Waiting to meet Oscar Mala Suerte and my friend Victor, I decided to cross the street from the Plaza to the Casa de Fierro (The Iron House). Built and designed by Gustav Eiffel, it was originally part of the Paris Exhibition of 1889. It stood next to the famous Eiffel Tower and other buildings. Imported from France in sections and assembled here in Iquitos during the rubber boom of the late 1800s, the Iron House symbolizes a time long gone. A brief moment in history when Iquitos and her "Rubber Barons" brought wealth and fame to this impoverished part of the world.

Opposite the Iron House stands the government office and small businesses selling passport and ID photos. Mala Suerte had lost his ID card. He would need to apply for duplicate documents, obtain photos and spend best part of the day lining-up inside. It reminded me of those long lines outside the immigration office at the Federal Building in

Downtown Los Angeles. Only honest people and dummies lined-up. Anyone with half a brain walked across the street to the parking lot in front of the Seven Eleven where you could buy good quality passports, birth certificates and green cards. Plus you could get a soda or a cup of coffee while waiting for the forgers to return!

On the corner of the Iron House vendors sold cigarettes, sodas and newspapers. A small stand sold empanadas. Originating from Argentina, stuffed with vegetables and meat, they are a cross between a pie and a sandwich - a sand-pie! In the corner on the sidewalk was baby in a box! As I looked at the child, he smiled. Far from looking sick and undernourished this boy appeared to be well-fed. But where were his parents? Several sand-pies later, Victor arrived. Victor thought the dad was the newspaper vendor on the corner. People passed-by, few if any even noticed the box, let alone the child within. A group of tourists took pictures of the baby boy before rushing-off to take pictures of monkeys and pink dolphins.

It was lunchtime and Oscar was still inside the Municipal Building. Sitting in the restaurant on the upper balcony of the Casa Fierro, I looked across the Plaza. But wait a minute, wasn't that Oscar walking over toward the box? Lifting the little boy out of the box he hugged him and then placed him back inside. It was a "father's hug!" Running-back down the steps I tried to attract Oscar's attention but it was too late. He had disappeared back inside the Municipal Building. I glanced inside at the multitude hoping to see him amongst the throng, but Mala Suerte was nowhere to be found.

Bristling with curiosity I took a mototaxi across town with Victor. We would go visit Oscar's Mum, she would surely know. Oscar's mother lived in a stilt house. The River Amazon rises some forty feet during the winter months. During the summer, the local kids and adults, play soccer on the ground beneath the stilt houses, but now the Amazon was high. The soccer patch was underwater and many houses could only be reached by canoe. A short canoe ride and we were at the wooden ladder that ascended upwards toward the door.

The Bar and Restaurant on the upper-level of the Casa de Fierro (The Iron House) looking -over the Plaza de Armas, Iquitos, Peru.

Oscar's mother, sister and brother at their stilt-house on the River Amazon

Oscar Mala Suerte (bad luck). In the Plaza de Armas, Iquitos.

As I entered the wooden structure I could see Oscar's Mum sitting on a bench at the far side. Sitting next to her was Oscar's little brother and sister. There was a gaping hole in the center of the room, planks were missing. Beneath the house the piranha infested waters swirled and churned. Oscar's brother held a fishing pole! Yes, Oscar had a baby. The mother had left to go work in Lima over a thousand miles away. Oscar's Mum would look after the baby if we brought it around. Before returning to the Plaza I went shopping with Victor for baby food and clothes.

Returning with Victor to the Plaza I heard someone calling me. It was Cheverenge the cigarette vendor. "Hi Cheverenge, I'm waiting for Oscar. He's been in the municipal building all day long, the line's so long. Now I think we'll have to return tomorrow." "Barry, why don't you go talk to the barman? He's holding Oscar's ID Card." "But Mala Suerte told me he'd lost his ID in the river." "No Barry. He went out drinking with friends on his birthday. They couldn't pay for the beers so the barman kept his ID. Oscar can get it back anytime he wants, but first he needs to pay for the beers he drank!" "So we've wasted a whole day at the municipality offices when all we needed to do was pay the barman for a few beers!" "No Barry, not a few beers. A few cases of beer!"

"Oscar, it's your child isn't it?" "Well, yes, but I don't want people to know. How did you find out?" "Your Mom and little sister told me. Why didn't you tell me the mother's abandoned you both and you needed to work to feed your child? That's why you needed to replace your ID card." "But Barry, I didn't think you would understand, being a Gringo and everything." "Well Oscar, I raised my son on my own from age four. I know exactly what it's like - to be abandoned. Let's go take a motokaro over to your mother's place, drop the baby-off and then go talk to the Barman!"

In California the discovery of a baby in a box would have been turned into a major media event. Police would scour the surrounding city looking for someone to arrest, anyone to arrest. The cardboard box would be cordoned-off with yellow tape and senior officers wearing badges and hats would take turns standing sentry. Police technicians, dusting for finger-prints, would examine the box for evidence of blood and DNA. The poor little child would be subjected to multiple swab tests for sexual abuse. Famous TV personalities would stand in front of the tiny box pleading for donations, even though they shipped their own kids off to boarding-school at age three and hadn't seen them since! Charities across the State, looking for publicity and donations would seize on the event. Mountains of clothes, shoes and diapers would arrive by mail overwhelming the local postal service. A special fund would be set-up to pay for the child's college tuition and thousands of childless couples would file legal challenges claiming the child belonged to them!

But this is Iquitos. Rainforest People live a peaceful, tranquil lifestyle. Why should they get caught-up in the California Vortex? After all, he was just a "**Baby in a Box!**"

ADRENALIN RAFTING
Great Amazon River Raft Race

Barry Seymour Brett

I've often wondered what kind of person would set about navigating the River Amazon on a raft. There was that nut back in the fifties who crossed the Atlantic on a raft. Then there was "Ben Hur" on that raft with the Roman Consul, "Row-well and Live". The Amazon? All those crazy piranhas swimming about. Aren't rafts held together with rope or something? Gnaw-gnaw! My good friend Mick had invited me to join the "Great Amazon Raft Race." It was his creation. Now I know why they call him "Mad Mick!" Having organized raft races in England many years ago he promotes the annual "Great Amazon Raft Race" here in Iquitos, Peru. Fifteen foreign teams and twenty-four Peruvian Teams would be competing.

City of Nauta. Early afternoon. "It's time to leave Barry. We're going-out to watch them construct their rafts." "But I've been bitten by something, my head aches." "It's swelling-up". "Don't worry Barry it's just an "Angochupo". "It's going to get worse before it gets better" "She's laid her eggs under your scalp. After a few days the worms hatch-out and leave!" "But I need to rest" "Barry, we have to go over to the Island to watch the teams construct their rafts NOW." "We need to determine the odds!" "The odds!" "What is this place?" "A betting parlor, a floating Casino on the Amazon?" "Miguel's holding the pot Barry, do you want in?"

As I watched the teams constructing their rafts I wondered what qualifications are required to man them. Do they have to pass a test in a swimming pool or a bathtub? Would they need a "Rafting License", or a "Diploma and Smog Certificate" from the Admiralty? Could contestants cheat? What about gigantic paddles and hollow logs! Could they lash-out at each other with horsewhips whilst shredding their opponent's logs with revolving can-openers? Or maybe there just aren't any rules at all!

But what's that? Coils of metal wire, a Black and Decker Chainsaw! Hammer and Nails made in China! I thought contestants were supposed to construct their rafts using only local materials. Neanderthals used a stone on a stick. Maybe Neanderthals had primitive brains but at least they were smart enough NOT to race rafts on the Amazon.

Lifejackets were to be worn at all times and no alcohol or drugs were permitted "ON THE RAFTS." Teams were allowed to hire local labor to aid in the construction of their rafts. A minimum of eight logs were required, but according to Mick, any configuration was permitted. The most common combination (commanding the best odds) was four logs in front linked to four behind. Linkage was everything. Some teams employed large screws, others used overlapping timbers bound together with metal wire. Three cross-beams were bound with rope to the main logs and plastic chairs with foam seating were common. Teams had numbers (for easy betting), and names. This would be "Gringa Linda's" third Great Amazon Raft Race. Her team called themselves "Vamos Ya" (Let's Go Right Now).

Carrying one of eight logs to construct the raft

Using Tools of Modern Man!

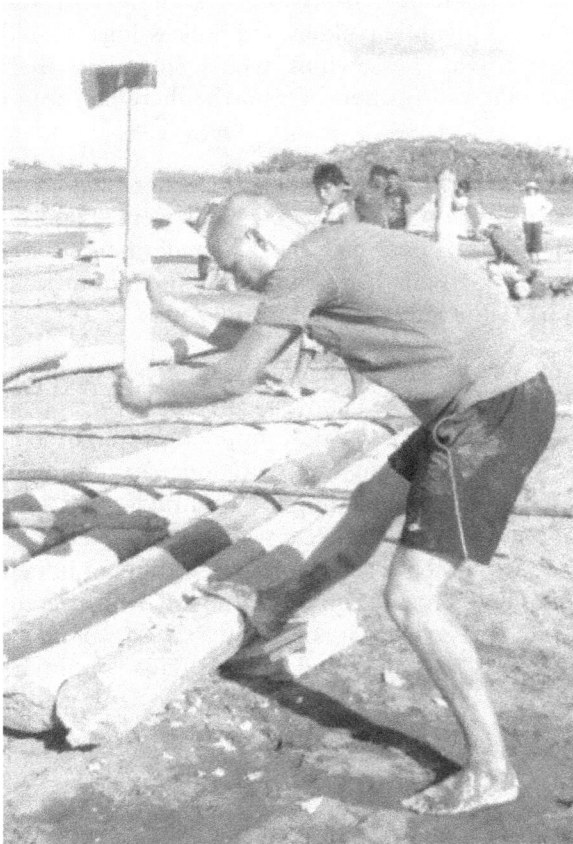

The favorites (5 to 1), were "Los Invensibles de Padre Cocha". An all Peruvian team, they had won several races before. There were teams named "Coca Loco", "Amazon Quest", "Los Titanes", "Los Increibles" (the Incredible), "Amazonia" and "Las 4 Virgenes de Ivalu" (Four Virgins of Ivalu). As a non-swimmer my favorite was "Don't Drown!" There were all-male teams, all female teams and mixed teams. Some team members volunteered to join only days before the start. Drinking a few beers in a London Pub, Tim overheard three crewmen crying in their beer. They were one member short. "Count me in!" he exclaimed. After a few more beers they carried him to the plane!

City of Nauta on the Amazon, eight in the morning "Barry, there's going to be a short delay." "The Chief Harbor Master wants to start the race!" "He wants the glamour!" "But he's drunk" "Wasn't he at the fiesta dancing with a hooker?" "Can he shoot straight?" "Does he have any ammo?" "Can I trade my lifejacket for a bullet proof vest?"

City of Nauta on the Amazon eight thirty in the morning. "It's number 18 at the gate, and they're off. 23's in the lead and it's "Vamos Ya" followed by "Coca Loco" and "Timbercreek." As they round the turn it's the "Four Virgins" followed by "Amazonia". The "Amazonians" are standing up! Californian surfers no doubt. "Hang Ten Guys, Surfs-Up." Oh gosh, are they FLASHING IT? Coming into the final stretch it's "Coca Loco" followed by "Vamos Ya" and "Kindred Spirits," and now it's "The Titans" and the "FOUR VIRGINS" followed closely by the "Four Flashers". The "Four Flashers" are gaining. The "Flashers" are Down! Now they're up - WAY-WAY UP!!! Neck and neck! They're coming "UP FROM BEHIND", now they're "UP ON THE INSIDE!" As they approach the finish line it's the "TWO VIRGINS" followed by the "FOUR FLASHERS" and "Vamos Ya" (Let's go Right Now!).

Mike Collis standing with the Amazon Jungle Drum Band

Linking the logs together to form a raft three logs wide

The Beachhead at the pueblo of Nueva Esperanza end of day two. At the top of the muddy hill a welcoming band playing Amazonian Drums greeted the arriving rafters. First one in, number 33 "Keepin' off Rio." Losing my foothold, trying to get closer to Mick and the VIPs, I slipped and rolled down the embankment into the mudbath below. "No I didn't, you sick S.O.B." "It's mud!" "What's that, a Mud Freak?"-"I'm a VIP" "African Chieftains smother their bodies with mud. - If it's good enough for them." "Anyway it's got medicinal properties." As I peered through the mud I could see "Los Increibles", "Gringa Linda with Vamos Ya" and "Lobo Marino de Nanay". Rafters arriving in high spirits spent the night dancing in the small discotheque and sleeping in the encampment above the cliffs.

Day Three. The Race to Tamshiyacu. This would be the longest and most difficult stretch. Rafters could be seen desperately searching for the current. Without the current they would suffer unbearable pain and exhaustion with the sun beating down on them. From the VIP boat we could see rafters, adrenalin pumping through their veins, as they tried to maintain speed. "Los Invensibles" were in the lead for the second day in a row, but who was that flying the Jolly Roger? "Piratas del Amazonas' (Pirates of the Amazon). On an adrenaline rush, the rafts-men paddled at lightning speed as the "Coca Leaf Tea" and "Bark Nectar" kicked-in!

We reached the junction in the river. Rafts were to proceed through the short-cut. No-one told them. Mick and other VIPs left the boat to establish a traffic control spot further along the beachhead. "We've got a red flag Barry, someone's in trouble." We have to leave now." "No time to pick-up Mick." "But they're without water in all this heat!" I exclaimed. "We've got to leave now" Ed screamed, as the Captain started the engine. But where were the Peruvian Coast Guard? They were to patrol the river to aid distressed rafts. Lunch-break. They had left for the day! Doubling-back some twenty minutes, a raft could be seen bobbing up and down while the rafts-men tried desperately to outmaneuver the strong current and bring-it alongside. The crew was exhausted. Suffering from dehydration, finally they realized they needed a tow.

"We've got another red flag" someone shouted, as the VIPs raced up-deck for a photo-shoot. "Everyone's rushing to the same side" Ed shouted, as the vessel lurched. "She's going to capsize." "Capsize!" "But I'm a VIP" "I can't swim". "At least I'd have a chance on a raft. Logs float." "Put your life-jacket on Barry" "The boat's caught in a strong current" My mind raced-back to that day-trip at Niagara Falls. "Goodbye lifejacket, I need a barrel! "But where were the rafts? "Oh they're way behind us now." So that's it. The race was fixed all along! The "VIP Boat's in the lead now." We're going to "Win!

Later that evening, in a Tamshiyacu bar, one of the female team members shared her diary with me. Desperately trying to take their minds of the pain and exhaustion they sang and paddled to "Christmas Carols" and "Queen's" "Bohemian Rhapsody." A song about a poor boy about to die. **"I'm just a poor boy, nobody loves me." "Too late, my time has come." "Sometimes I wish I'd never been born at all!"** What about **"We are the Champions!" "No Time for Losers".** There were other notations. The desperate need to propel the raft with long deep strokes, and the struggle to maintain speed in the wake of passing vessels. The routine of constantly changing sides to relieve the pressure on one arm. Bathroom breaks that involved standing or squatting at the rear of the raft. There were unforgettable moments such as when a young boy rolled a water-melon down the embankment to help quench their thirst. The kids sitting on a riverside bank shouting down to them "They make motors now!" "Then there was the realization that for them, it had nothing to do with coming in **first,** or even **last,** but everything to do with **not being towed!** Towing was the ultimate humiliation.

Day Four. The last lap was grueling. Facing a fierce current along the Nanay River, rafts inched along toward the finish line. Crewmen who failed to paddle in unison found their raft going backwards as the current dragged them back toward the Amazon. "Didn't someone say **The Current is Your Friend?"** "With friends like that? As the local saying goes "The Amazon has the River but the Nanay has the Current." Three crewmen fainted and others found themselves towed-in. Is that the "Pirates of the Amazon" being towed? Ran-out of Coca Leaves and Bark Nectar? Good thing they don't have to "walk the plank!" Rafting Teams were totally exhausted as they crossed the finish line. Team members posing for photo-shoots collapsed on their decks or suffered humiliation as they fell from their rafts into the water, only to be dragged onshore by young boys. The revenge of the Incas I thought as Los Increibles, the "Peruvian Victors," crossed the finish line.

At least I now know what kind of person races a raft on the Amazon looking for the ultimate "Adrenalin Rush." The same kind of person who climbs Mount Everest, Explores Antarctica or walks on the Surface of the Moon (or lives in the Rainforest!). A Crazy Human!

Ayahuasca High

Barry Seymour Brett

Thousands of tourists descend on Iquitos and the surrounding jungle each year to experience ayahuasca (eye-ah waska). Some tourists visit the jungle city every year for the sole purpose of hiring a Shaman to perform the ayahuasca ceremonies. Once a year a group of two hundred foreign tourists arrive for the ayahuasca symposium. A strange bunch indeed. Most look like they'd never heard of makeup, or visited a barber or hairdresser. On a California beach they would be arrested for vagrancy!

Gene, an acquaintance whom I had met on the Amazon Boulevard, decided he wanted to try the ayahuasca experience. Afraid he could get ripped-off he asked me to accompany him for the ceremony. Ben, a teacher in a local school and Gene's best friend Lenny also wanted to experience the ayahuasca high. This was to be Gene's last fling. He was about to marry Rosa, a young waitress working in my bar.

We met at my bar on the Amazon Boulevard. Leaving in a mototaxi we drove for almost an hour down muddy pathways to a remote jungle area. Already dark and without street lighting it was difficult to find the Shaman's house. I would not be partaking of the ceremony, but would sit-in as an observer. We had heard of people being ripped-off, raped (male and female) and some people had drowned in their own excrement!

There was a small hut toward the far-end of the backyard. To the side of the hut was a stone bench. At the other end of the yard someone had dug a long trench. We all sat-down in the hut while the Shaman chanted the magic words and phrases. He didn't really look like a Shaman. Wearing "Billabong Shorts" and a baseball cap embroidered with "Mick Jagger's Lips" he could have been riding a board under Huntington Beach Pier! Where was the wand and the pointed hat? The bone through the nose and the jungle paint? The chants were in Spanish and long and difficult to follow. I thought of my Church Pastor back in Huntington Beach, California. His sermons could be long and difficult to follow, and he preached in English!

Whilst chanting, the Shaman prepared the special brew. It was thick and stodgy with oily black streaks. Something like "Manhattan Clam Chowder sprinkled with WD40!" But without the crackers and the oil can. The streaks are from the hallucinogenic herb chiric sanango. Gene was the first to drink the potion. Lenny and Ben followed suit. Smoking mapacho jungle tobacco wrapped inside toe (toe-way) leaves, the Shaman proceeded to blow it into their faces. The toe leaf is an hallucinogenic leaf extracted from ayahuasca vine wood. The power of the ayahuasca ceremony is derived from the ikaros, the songs the shaman chants as he blows the smoke. The ikaros sing of the relationship between God and the Spirits of the Jungle. Twenty minutes later and still nothing happened. The chanting continued and we all made jokes about the whole ceremony being a rip-off. "I want my money-back" Gene screamed as he proceeded to strip naked and dance around the small hut! "Hold my Hand" Lenny whimpered as he rushed out the door and threw-up. A few minutes later Ben curled-up on the floor in the fetal position and cried.

Lenny and Gene danced naked around the small courtyard. Ben ran-out the door and rushed-over to the trench. Dropping his pants there was a horrible gush. It sounded as if everything had been sucked-out of him with a giant plunger. "Hold my hand Barry, hold my hand." "Are you kidding, look where it's been?" One hell of a laxative, I thought. I'll never buy an enema at Walmart's again. All I need is a bowl of Clam Chowder and a can of WD40!

Lenny and Gene sat naked on the stone bench, hugging each other as they whimpered. Ben's voice sounded like he'd just left a helium tent. All this time the Shaman continued to chant. Ben climbed a tree and made bird noises for an hour or so. Several hours went-by. Gene and Larry crawled along the ground desperately searching for the overflowing trench. Why bother I thought. There was moonlight but nevertheless it was difficult to see. "Barry, help us to the trench" "Are you crazy Gene, I could slip and fall!" Squelch, squelch! "Can't you smell your way over there?" Larry fell face-down into the trench. Fearing he might drown I squelched my way over to the stinking trench. As I pulled him out I was reminded of those camouflaged marines in Vietnam.

As I waited for the potion to wear-off, I cast my mind back to that overland trip to San Francisco many years ago. Everyone was looking for a new high. "Put a flower in your hair". Haight Ashbury was the street of hallucinations. Young teens smoked weed and sat down in a daze or giggled over nothing. Acid trippers stared and quivered. No-one climbed a lamp post, made bird noises, threw up in trenches or danced naked in the street!

Ben was the first to snap-out of the coma! "Let's go back to the hotel" he whispered with his helium-balloon voice. "You're butt-naked and your clothes are soiled!" "I'll wear Gene's pants." Wrapping Gene and Lenny in a blanket we left for the hotel in a motokaro. As we left I glanced inside the Shaman's house. I could see his family watching a skateboarding movie on TV while the "Rolling Stones" blasted-out "Brown Sugar". Good business I thought as I noticed he was the only house on the block with electricity and a motor bike.

The following afternoon I returned to their hotel to check things out. Lenny was sleeping on the shower room floor and Gene was under the table. Ben was alert and cooking hot dogs in the kitchen. "How was it Ben?" "I don't remember much but I feel wonderful now." "I've never felt so good in my life before." "All my anxieties and worries have left me." "I feel so clean" Maybe I could hold his hand now I thought! Able to smell his way around now, and lured by the aroma of hot dogs on the grill, Gene climbed-out from under the table. "Barry, I feel awesome, it's like my whole life's starting over again" "All the poisons and all the frustrations and burdens of a lifetime have suddenly vanished. By-the-way, I'm postponing the wedding". "Oh no, Rosa will be upset. What about her family, they've been planning this wedding for weeks?" "Barry, I'm going to do ayahuasca again next week!" "I feel renewed and refreshed". "To think of all that money I wasted on acid and mushrooms" "If only I had known!"

Back in the States, driving down Ventura Highway, I noticed a "Kragen Auto Parts". Feeling miserable and down after another round in the divorce court, I pulled into the lot. Leaving the automotive store I walked over the street to the seafood restaurant. "Manhattan Clam Chowder to go please". "Would you like some crackers sir?" "No, that's fine; I've got **"everything"** I need!"

Nazca Seedlings

Barry Seymour Brett

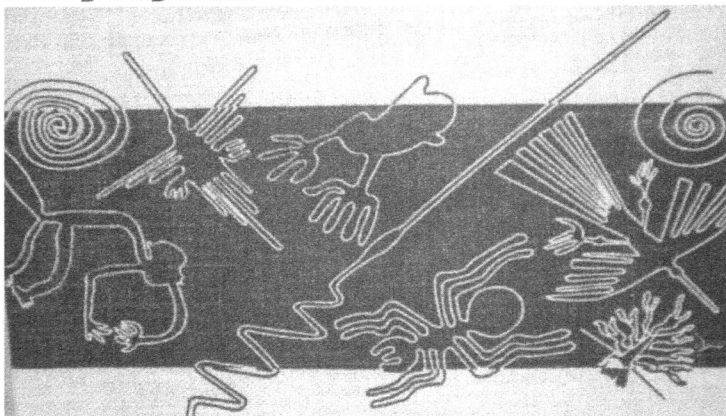

Nazca Line paintings

Like most people who visit the Nazca Lines, I had read all kinds of crazy tales concerning their origin. Who were these artisans and what is the significance of their designs? There were the usual boring theories about ancient Nazca cultures put-out by world renowned archaeologist who couldn't find a weed in their own backyard! Then there were the popular "Ancient Astronaut" theories". Destitute authors trying to make a buck have described how the Nazca Lines were in fact giant landing strips. Ancient astronauts were supposed to have landed there to **"sow their seeds!"** If so they must have lost their way or ran-out of gas. Someone mentioned that it hadn't rained on Nazca for five-thousand years! It was the absence of rain that has enabled the etchings to survive in tact. Since all known life forms require water, what kind of Astronaut would chose to land there? Only a **"Penniless Author"** would pick a waterless desert as a landing strip!

A mile or so out-of-town stood a viewing tower. Built years ago by a German archaeologist, tourists climb upwards to view the hieroglyphs. Lacking altitude the tower was too short to provide a good view of the designs but was high enough to topple-over in a heartbeat! It looked a little like a mini-Eiffel Tower with a ladder, but felt like the Leaning Tower of Pisa! As I lined-up I noticed vendors selling warm sodas, cigarettes and stale cakes. A young boy rented-out binoculars. I wanted to rent a safety harness but I couldn't see one.

As we climbed toward the top I could see brief outlines of some of the less interesting designs. A guide (from Planet Mars?) stood at the top. Describing a particular formation, viewers rushed to one side as the tower lurched and vultures circled above! The ladder was barely wide enough for one person. People climbing-up would be greeted by people coming-down! It was a "friendly crunch!" The rented binoculars proved useless. My son's kaleidoscope would have provided a better image. Not that there was much of interest to see. The surrounding terrain resembled a lunar landscape with nothing but rocks and fine sand. People who couldn't afford the flights thought it was great.

Several planes sat on the tarmac. They were all four or six-seaters. A burnt-out plane sat at the far end of the runway! "There's nothing to worry about sir" "All the pilots are experienced (licensed?)". Flying in a four-seater with two other tourists I was amazed at how skilled the pilot really was. The plane was highly maneuverable making several deep dives through the mist and clouds. Constantly banking to provide good camera shots of the hieroglyphs, the pilot had what it took. There was a design resembling a **"Spaceman"** wearing his helmet and nearby an outline of a **"Monkey."** "Planet of the Apes" maybe? No. It couldn't have been them. Charlton Heston taught them to fly a **"paper-plane**." Those Apes were way "behind the curve!" We nosedived and took a sharp turn toward the **"Giant Bird"**. They got that wrong! Anyone could see it was a **"Romulan Spaceship"**. Captain Kirk - even my son knows that!

The fact of the matter is that many of the so-called designs are solely in the minds of the beholder. Two people looking at the same symbol could reach different interpretations as to what it represented. As we flew above the **"Nike Logo"** toward the **"Coca Cola Man"** it was getting hazy and difficult to see. Just when I thought I'd seen it all, there she was, staring at me through the misty haze. Just an outline of a toothless jutting-jaw and twisted nose. **"Mother-in-Law!"** So she really was an Alien! Is there no way to get away from her, not even out in the Cosmos! "Pilot turn the Starship around, warp speed - time to get out of here!" Suddenly the engines cut. If the Nazca Lines represented giant landing strips we could sure use one now I thought, as the pilot scanned the horizon looking for the **"Gas Pump Symbol".** "Don't worry sir; we're trained to glide back-in!" Finally we touched-down. Walking away after prayers, I tried to visualize what those images really signified. It's hard to imagine super intelligent beings from another world scraping and carving patterns in the dirt with a trowel! Wouldn't they have atomic drills and laser-etchers? Even Superman has things like that and he lives here on Earth in Hollywood! Resembling stick-figures on a kindergarten wall, there's nothing graceful or artistic about their work. They must have been drop-outs from a cosmic art-school!

They weren't really all that advanced either. Not only did they pick a waterless desert to land in, they forgot to patent and trademark their designs. I guess they don't have logos or trademarks out there in the Cosmos, but they sure come in useful down here on Planet Earth. They missed-out on a small fortune. Hundreds of picture postcards, Tee-shirts and handbags embellished with symbols from the **"Nazca Lines".** Finally I've figured-out the mystery of the "Nazca Lines." They came from distant galaxies to warn us to shop **"Nike"** and drink **"Coca Cola."** We need to get our planet straightened out, otherwise we're doomed! If so the message fell on deaf ears. After all there are still countries left where people "don't speak English," and have "never" shopped at **Walmart** or **Seven-Eleven!** Those Aliens still have a lot of work to do "sowing their seeds". So maybe that's it. Why didn't I think of it before? We haven't been able to finish the job. So **"They're coming back!"**

The House that Jack Built

Barry Seymour Brett

Ernesto the Master Builder

Kicking back in my newly constructed house, I sipped coffee upstairs and peered-out the window at the jungle below. Relaxed and at ease, listening to "Musica Romantica", my thoughts drifted-back to Don Carlos the real estate agent. "Barry it's a steal, they have to move to Lima, they're desperate to sell." As I leaned-back into my cozy armchair I started to drift-off. Suddenly I woke-up with a jolt. Oh no, there it was again - Ernesto the Master Builder - his face in 3-D. Stuffing his pockets with greenbacks, taunting me, provoking me, grinning at me. The horrible chanting got louder and louder "three for me and one for Barry, one for Barry and three for me". The nightmare, the horror of it all. It was all coming-back to haunt me once again.

"The walls, I don't own the walls!" "Barry, only the front and back, the walls on either side belong to your neighbors". "So I've bought a piece of land with a corrugated roof straddling my neighbor's walls?" "Exactly, but don't worry we can fix it." "But how?" "We'll offer to buy a half-interest in your neighbor's walls. They're broke, we can bargain for a good price - but there's no water. We need to sink an artesian well." "A well! But we're four blocks from the River Amazon, the largest freshwater river in the world!" "The city pumps are too weak; I need water to mix the cement."

"Barry, I've got bad news". "No, not again, what is it this time Ernesto?" "The front wall, it's crumbling. We had to prop it up with timber." "Why?" "The bricks were held together with sand. The cement was mixed at ten bags of sand to one of cement - they were trying to save money." "Now I'll have to build a new front wall?" "Yes, and the back wall, its sandy too!" "Ernesto, are you telling me that I don't own any walls, just the land between?" "Barry, you own the roof!"

"I've screwed-up Barry, the door to your bedroom, it's too low. It's nothing to worry about; you'll just have to bend-your head to pass through!" "No Ernesto, you're the Master Builder, how could this have happened?" "Barry, you're a Gringo. Rainforest people are short and the door would be just fine for them." "By the way. The front door is worm-ridden we need to replace it!"

A knock at the temporary front door. The man from Electro-Oriente. "I need you to re-connect the power." "Sir, that'll be $50" As I handed the man the money he looked on in amazement. "Not now sir, you need to go down to the office and pay, anytime between now and the next six-months!" Wow, I thought, finally something I like about Peruvian Bureaucracy. They cut my power-off in California, and I was only one month in arrears.

As I looked at the new door I noticed it had no hinges and no doorknob. "They're extra; they weren't included in the quote". "What's with the bathroom Ernesto, there's no toilet or washbasin and no tiles!" "The quote was for the bathroom, not for the fittings!" "But it's not a bathroom without fittings! I thought the quote would include a toilet and tiles". "This is Peru, thinking is one thing, facts are something else. If you wanted a toilet and tiles you should have said so. Many Peruvians do without them!"

"Now what's wrong? Don't tell me. I bought the house from squatters and the real owner has just showed-up!" "No, no Barry, it's not that bad. We can't tile the living room floor, the cement won't set. The roof's rusty and leaking. We'll have to replace the roof!" "So that's it, no walls and now I have no roof. I own a piece of jungle land and nothing more!" A week passed-bye and still Electro Oriente had not connected the power. A trip to their office was in order. Arriving in a motokaro I noticed a large group of people out-front. A security guard stood by the door. "There's a power outage sir, it's closed for the day!" Returning the following morning I got straight down to the nitty gritty. "You told me you would re-connect and I had six months to pay". "Yes sir, that's correct. We'll be re-connecting you in six months time and then you need to pay us!"

Panoramic view of the Jungle from my upstairs window

Workers constructing my new roof

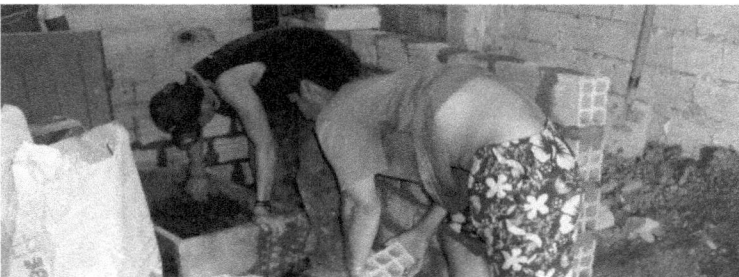

Bricklayers re-building the walls to my Jungle House

"Don't worry Barry, six months isn't very long, it'll soon pass bye. Many people in the city go without electricity for months at a time." "Out in the jungle areas they have no electricity at all, it's a minor inconvenience." "Minor inconvenience, but Ernesto we're four degrees off the Equator, I need a fan and a freezer." "Well OK, you're a Gringo, I know that. We can solve this tomorrow."

Nine in the morning, a knock at my new wormless, doorknob-less door. It was my good friend from Electro Oriente paying me a courtesy call. "Ernesto sent me. I need $100 up-front and $20 for each of my men - in cash." As I looked out through my "temporary window" I could see an Electro Oriente truck parked out-front. "Five men" carried a ladder and two men carried cable!

Three months passed bye and finally the day arrived. Celebrating with Ernesto and his work-crew, I thanked them all for the many hours they had spent constructing my house. Ernesto turned toward me. "My son's studying construction engineering. There's good money in construction." "Yes Ernesto, and even better money in demolition!"

Birthday Cake

Barry Seymour Brett

It was a small cake shop across the road from my friend Lewis's street stand. Lewis sold sunglasses and cell phone cases. We stood and talked for a while. It was Gabriel's eighteenth birthday. I was picking-up his cake. Lewis reminded me that his birthday was coming-up soon. As I entered the store a customer left in a motokaro carrying a chocolate cake. Various cakes were on display, but where was Gabriel's cake? "Excuse me, I ordered a chocolate birthday cake yesterday, I've come to pick-it-up." "We don't have any chocolate cakes sir, what name is it?" "It's a cake for Gabriel." "Oh, that cake. We just sold it to someone else. It's late, we are about to close and we didn't think you were coming!" "But I pre-paid" "Sir, we can give you your money back tomorrow." "What's wrong with right now?" "We don't have any cash in the till, Maria went to the bank." "Wait a minute you just sold Gabriel's cake, you must have the money." "We sold it at half price, just to get rid of it!" "I'm sorry sir, we need your business, it won't happen again."

"Walking back across the street I told Lewis what happened. "It's not too late Barry, I know the driver. He always parks his motokaro in front of the store waiting for customers carrying cakes. He'll be back; he knows all the cake stores in the City. Sure enough half an hour later he returned. Yes he did know of another cake shop across town. "Yes sir we have chocolate cake, but it's still in the oven." At least it will be fresh I thought. The driver would pick-up the cake later. I returned home.

It was late evening. Gabriel was at my door. "Cumpleaños Feliz Gabriel" (happy birthday). We sat and talked for a while and then I walked over to the refrigerator and removed the birthday cake. Knowing that many families in Iquitos can't afford the luxury of a birthday cake (nine or ten children per family is not unusual), I had thought Gabriel would want to take it home. But no, Gabriel had problems with his Dad. He would probably be beaten and his cake eaten before he had a chance to get a bite! He would celebrate his eighteenth birthday with me and I was to take a picture of the cake to show his mother and friends. My neighbors came round and we all sang the happy birthday song in Spanish. Suddenly Gabriel burst into tears. "Gabriel what's wrong?" "I'm sorry Barry; it's just that I've never had a birthday cake before. The candle and everything, it's just the shock."

I couldn't help but think about that wild birthday party at my neighbor's house in Huntington Beach., California. In the corner was a BMX bike wrapped with a large blue birthday bow. Someone had scrawled "Happy Birthday Son" on the large mirror behind the "Private Bar". It was difficult to see the birthday cake without stretching my neck and peering over mountains of food, bowls of ice-cream and chocolate mousse. Pizza boxes littered the floor as overweight kids wearing party hats chomped down on hamburgers and hot dogs as they sprayed each other with silly string. That entire charade for a teenager just out of juvenile hall, a high school drop-out with no future. Gabriel worked 6 to 4 carrying wood logs for his uncle. Wearing shoes held together with a paper-clip, he walked four miles everyday from his job to the college where he studied from 7 to 10 at night.

Early afternoon, I was preparing to go to the soccer match at Max Augustin Stadium. Someone was at the window. It was Howard and his younger brother Juan. I had stayed with them and their family at Barrio Florido, the tiny pueblo two hours down river. "Hi Barry, we're going to visit Howard's Aunt here in Iquitos. Can we sleep over at your place tonight?" "Yeah, sure, maybe we could all go to the watering hole (Pampachica) tomorrow." Juan grinned. "Wow Barry, that's a great idea, its Howard's nineteenth birthday tomorrow! On the way to the stadium I dropped-bye the cake shop. "Remember me?" "Yes sir, your chocolate cake will be ready tomorrow morning." "Don't forget, his name's Howard and he's an Allianza-Lima supporter. I want it iced with his name and the Allianza team colors."

Across the street was a store selling Piñatas. Most Californians would know what a Piñata was but for those readers unfamiliar with Hispanic traditions, a piñata is a papier-mâché figurine. Molded in the likeness of clowns, soccer balls, Barbie dolls and animals, they are brightly painted and filled with small gifts and confetti. The piñata is strung from the ceiling. Blindfolded revelers smash the Piñata with a stick and the gifts cascade to the ground.

Looking around the store there were many beautiful and very artistic piñatas molded into jungle animals and birds. Such a shame I thought, to batter them with a stick. I should look for an ugly one, something to vent my frustrations on. My divorce attorney came to mind. I've often felt like smashing him to pulp. This could be my chance, payback with a vengeance, but no such luck. There were ogres, red devils and phantoms but no divorce attorney!

Lewis the street vendor taken several weeks prior to the death of his baby girl.

Daniel holding the Pilsen Beer Bottle Piñata & Michael (La Gallina)

I finally settled on a "Pilsen Beer Bottle Piñata!" As I was about to leave the store I took a double-take. Surely not, but yes there it was, the ultimate pay-back - a bride and bridegroom piñata! I tried to imagine the wedding reception. "No I don't love you; I'm marrying you for the house and the car. Ouch, take that!" "Who am I marrying, you or your mother? Ouch, take that!"

Returning from Pampachica with Howard, Juan and friends we arrived at my house in festive mood. Daniel carried a case of beer on his shoulder as we entered. Michael came-bye and played Zamponya while Juan sang. Howard was blindfolded and after several failed attempts, finally smashed the Piñata to smithereens. Small gifts and confetti cascaded to the ground as everyone scrambled to retrieve them. Later that evening Michael played the happy birthday song on Zamponya while Daniel lit the candles on the cake. Howard cried. I didn't even ask what was wrong. I guess deep down inside I really knew.

Copyright November 2009

Fiesta in a Treetop

Barry Seymour Brett

As I sat outside a roadside café, a couple of neighborhood girls strolled-bye. They stopped and we chatted for a while. Rosa and Giselle were waiting for their boyfriends. They were planning a walk into the rainforest where they would meet other neighborhood youths. Would I care to join them? "Well, yes, but do I need anything?" "No Barry, you don't need anything, just come as you are. We don't have anything. No money or anything like that!" Giselle's boyfriend Elvis, (yes, Elvis is alive! - at least here in the jungle!), met us in the Plaza and soon we were joined by several other youths. Elvis's younger brother Marden, ran-over to his uncle's house to pick-up a machete. Some of the boys wanted me to buy them beer but I settled for a couple of bottles of alcoholic soda and bottled table-water. A few loaves of bread and some plastic cups and we were all set.

It was mid-morning, but the weather was fine, not too hot and humid, as Giselle's eight year-old cousin ferried us across the river in a small boat. Asking half a Sole (15cents), I gave him five. That would be more money than his family had seen all week. I sat in the boat next to Marden and his uncle's machete. It was almost as big as he was. We walked for best part of an hour, eventually reaching a small clearing. As we approached the clearing I could hear singing and then someone called-out my name. "Barry, Barry, ven, ven (over here)." It was Miguel, the cement man who had worked on my house with the Master-Builder, Ernesto. Miguel was perched with some friends way-up above us in a large tree overlooking the clearing. Straddling the boughs, Miguel and three other youths played card games. One of the guys on the ground carried a soccer ball, but Marden, Elvis's twelve year-old brother, would need to clear the undergrowth first with his uncle's machete. Thrashing the undergrowth furiously, I was afraid he might seriously harm someone - me! No-one seemed the least bit bothered as Elvis handed him a cup of the alcoholic soda! "No, no, Elvis, Marden's a bit too young." "Come-on Barry, don't worry, he drinks bark-nectar wine with his dad at weekends!" "OK, just a sip or two" As he took a drink I checked the ground for severed limbs!

Rosa's boyfriend helped her climb an adjacent tree, but her ancestors were rubber tree tappers and so she really didn't need any help. It looked like a breeze! I went apple-picking once in a small village in Kent, Southeastern England, but those English kids were so far behind the curve they had to use ladders! The apple trees were nothing more than small bushes when compared to the great rainforest trees. If you want to go broke in the Amazon, just try selling ladders or elevators! There were two other girls sitting on the branches with their boyfriends. Elvis and Raymondo climbed-up, balancing the sodas and other goodies on their shoulders. I wanted to join them but I never was much of a climber. Machu Picchu, the Statue of Liberty, Leaning Tower of Pisa - but they had steps! Apple trees with a ladder - yes. I did climb the Great Pyramid of Egypt once back in the sixties. But I had youth on my side back then. Miguel, realizing my dilemma, climbed-down from his perch, crossed over to our tree and helped me-up.

Kids moved-over to make room for me on a large branch. Sitting next to a boy with his mp3 Discman, I noticed something was missing. "Batteries!" Without money and living in extreme poverty, imagination plays a dynamic role in their lives. Youths took turns holding the Discman and putting the ear-buds into their ears. Singing imaginary songs they would tap-out a beet as the branch swayed to the rhythm. Pouring-out the "sodas," I gazed down at the spectacular view below. Our tree was higher than most and I could catch glimpses of the scenery all the way down to the Nanay River.

Raymondo's grandpa showed-up with two neighbors and a bottle of rum! Guys stood foot-on-shoulder, lifting grandpa up to the lower branches. They could get a spot at Ringling Brother's Circus I thought. More youths arrived and occupied another tree. They brought more "sodas" and some juanes (rice balls with chicken, wrapped in palm leaves). Elvis leaned-over toward me. "How do you like Wendy? I'm in love with her" "Wendy? I thought her name was Giselle." "No Barry, not Giselle, I'm talking about the tree." "Wendy the tree, I'm in love with her". It didn't take long to realize that all the trees had names. The kids knew all the trees, the type of species, and how old they were.

Rainforest kids are at one with the trees that surround them. Trees are very much part and parcel of who they are and their very existence depends upon their relationship with the rainforest trees. "But Raymondo, don't you cut them down with machetes for firewood and to make charcoal?" "Barry, this is the rainforest, within a year or two the trees grow-back!" "Look at Marden. He's clearing the undergrowth, but in a week or two when we return the undergrowth will be thick again and difficult to pass." "If we ever need to fell "Wendy", we'll hold a ceremony first with the local Shaman. We need to share her pain before she sacrifices her life for us."

As I admired the view from atop of "Wendy", some of the boys and girls imitated various jungle bird sounds. Calling to each other from adjacent trees, they would tease each other with a variety of bird mating calls. Chirp, chirp - I love your plume. Warble, warble - I'd love to ruffle your feathers. Squawk squawk - let's nest together. Hoot, hoot - let's make eggs!

One of the older boys played zamponya as Raymondo's grandpa and several girls and boys began to sing. I recognized the tune. Michael (La Gallina) and his brother Julio had played it at their family's Christmas dinner the previous year. I had shot a video-clip with my camera and knew the words, so we all sang together. Miguel and his friends, sitting in "Margarita", an adjacent tree, joined-in the sing-song. It was one of those wonderful fleeting moments, but how could I possibly explain this to American youths whose partying experience got no further than a California Beach BBQ or a Rooftop Party in Downtown Manhattan. Would they have invited grandpa and his neighbors plus a twelve year-old boy carrying a machete? Would grandpa and his neighbors have accepted the invitation? There is no divide between young and old amongst the rainforest peoples.

The boy with the battery-less Discman told me his Dad was a tree-tapper for many years until he had a motorbike accident. Unable to work and without any other source of income the family had slipped into extreme poverty. He had climbed trees as a tapper with his dad and older brothers since age four! "My brother works for a cable company. They climb five story buildings to install cable - without a ladder!"
Later in the day some of the boys played soccer in the clearing while others sat in the tall trees and watched. As I looked down at them from "Wendy" I thought about what we in the West have lost. Trees are scenic artifacts to most of us. People who show compassion toward

trees are casually dismissed as "tree huggers". We don't view trees as living vibrant entities, and certainly we don't give them all names.

I recalled that giant sequoia in, Northern California, many years ago. Spectacular as it was, I don't recall anyone telling me the sequoia had a name, as I drove my pick-up through its' hollowed-out center with my son. The park warden didn't tell me he wanted to share its' pain even though with a gaping hole that size I'm sure it must have felt something! It didn't seem like the park warden was in love with it, or with anything else for that matter, other than maybe his paycheck and pension! It was just a tourist trinket, a photo-op on a picture postcard.

After the soccer game Marden cleared a pathway down to a small lake where the youths, boys and girls, grandpa and his adult friends bathed naked. There was no shame, no giggling, and no embarrassment. No-one hid behind a rock. This was part of normal everyday life. As natural as breathing.

Dusk was soon approaching and the mosquitoes would start to swarm. It was time to say goodbye to "Margarita and Wendy" and march-back toward the city behind Marden the machete wielding twelve year-old! As we trekked down the narrow pathway, I thought about my own son. I would not have trusted him with a machete at age twelve, not even with the lawn mower! Yet this lad swung it with precision and skill, even after swigging the booze! A twelve year-old carrying a machete down Main Street (or any street) Huntington Beach would have been immediately arrested and put in Juvenile Hall. Probably charged with carrying a dangerous weapon! Even though the danger clearly depends, not on the weapon, but on whose brandishing it. Something has happened to us, that's for sure. Californians willingly give-up their freedoms for comfort and perceived security.

Young children in Europe and North America are prevented from working. Deprived of the opportunity to work and support the family unit, children lose their worth. With nothing of value to offer they become actors and actresses without a role, drifting script-less away from responsible behavior into the abyss of video games, drugs and juvenile delinquency. Rudderless and without real value to the family, they deteriorate and become nothing more than artifacts, adorable pets and trophies.

We've lost confidence in ourselves and in our children. 150 years ago in Northern California, the Donner Party, stranded in a blizzard and dying of starvation sent a twelve year-old boy across the snow covered peak of what is now called the "Donner Pass" in search of help. They had confidence in him. He fought his way on foot through 100 miles of snow and blizzard to arrive at the Sacramento Fort and summon help.

Somewhere in California. "Honey what's wrong?" "It's Danny he's missing again." "Let's check the GPS - oh there he is, across the street at the Robinsons". "I don't like this dear, he's not really old enough to be crossing the street on his own." "Well honey, maybe it's time to teach him a lesson. Let's threaten to cancel his birthday party next week." "Yes, that'll make him think twice before he crosses over to the Robinsons' again" "He's really looking forward to his twenty-first!"

Carnival Rio

Barry Seymour Brett

Statue of Jesus Christ the Redeemer overlooking the harbor in Rio de Janeiro, Brazil.

As a Christian arriving in Rio, one of the first things I wanted to do was visit the statue of "Jesus Christ the Redeemer." Standing on the top of a hill overlooking the city, the statue of Jesus towers over the surrounding harbor. Catching a cab, it was a long winding drive to the assembly area. There were gift shops selling picture postcards and souvenir statues. It brought back memories of that first visit to Liberty Island. Whereas the "Statue of Liberty" was larger and more beautiful, nevertheless "Jesus Christ the Redeemer" was impressive and awe-inspiring. The sad truth is that the "Magnificent City" that erected "Liberty" whilst proclaiming freedom, would in the name of freedom never tolerate a statue of Jesus Christ"

"Oh yeh, Oh yeh." "The statue of Jesus Christ on Liberty Island, make your donations here." "Oh, thank you sir. What's inside, a check, a wad of bills?" "A court writ, a summons!" "The Supreme Court?"

"He has to stand next to a statue of the Buddha and Elvis Presley!" "But, Elvis? He's still alive, isn't he?" "The league for Fairness in the Media, who are they? "Next to the Devil?" "But your honor, there's no room on Liberty Island for all these statues." "The committee for people of color. What do you mean; paint Jesus half-black and half white standing next to a statue of Michael Jackson!" "But Michael Jackson, he was white - wasn't he?"

Unlike New York City, the people of Rio de Janeiro are proud of their statue of Jesus towering above them. Tourists and business travelers are encouraged, pressured to go visit. Escalators carry visitors up to the Statue from the assembly area. Standing at the top of the hill and at the base of the Statue I could see the entire harbor, including Sugar Loaf Mountain and the world famous beach of Copacabana.

Outside the Sambadromo, scalpers were selling tickets. For $100 I was assured of first class deluxe seating. A young boy approached. For $20 dollars I could go-over to his Granny's house and watch the parade from her balcony. Walking down the alley to "Granny's House" I noticed a small balcony in the distance. Overflowing with people "Granny's Balcony" shook and vibrated. Not wanting to be the "straw that broke the Camel's back" I decided to return to the scalpers. But where was the deluxe seating? The seats were nothing more than concrete steps. There were no numbers, people squeezed-in. More people arrived and everyone squeezed a little tighter. There was a loud gasp, as two grossly overweight Americans arrived and tried to take their place!

The carnival procession started at nine at night and lasted through to six in the morning! The climate was hot and humid.. "Granny's Deluxe Balcony" took on new meaning as we stood like sardines in a row. I assumed that as the night wore-on spectators would start to leave and head-back to their hotels. No such luck. The processions and displays were breathtaking in their magnificence. Only a total loser would contemplate leaving early. So dynamic and entertaining were the parades that when I finally made a trip to the restroom I was afraid of missing something. It would be next to impossible to describe the extravaganza in words. In sum total it was Pasadena Rose Parade, Times Square on New Year's Eve and New Orleans at Mardi Gras, all rolled into one!

Standing in front of the panoramic view of Rio de Janeiro.

Magnificent displays of color and dance dominated the nine-hour extravaganza

A never-ending display of beautiful costumes paraded in front of me

The costumes were magnificent and all the participants danced to the special theme music composed each year for this gigantic spectacle. There were hundreds of floats depicting various themes. The lead-float depicted scenes from Star Wars, complete with Darth Vader brandishing a light saber and fifty or more R2 D2s dancing and bobbing about. There were floats dressed-up as jungle scenes. Dancers were all dressed in brightly colored costumes. The more exotic costumes must have taken months to design and prepare. Visitors from other parts of Brazil, together with foreigners, were permitted (encouraged) to participate.

Identical costumes could be rented at various locations several days before the procession kicked-off. Many of the magnificent costumes were designed by famous artists and employ felt, cotton and colored fabrics together with brightly painted ostrich feathers. Visitors renting costumes were expected to "Blend-in" with the procession as it wound its way along the oblong stadium. Brazilians, like their Rainforest cousins in Peru, were born with the dance in them. Anyone who has spent time in South America knows only too well that North Americans including the transplanted "People of Color" have totally lost it, when it comes to dancing. The "Whites" never ever had it to begin with!" So what's with "Blending-In". Visitors "Blending-in" were nothing less than an eyesore in an otherwise perfect display of pageantry.

"Honey wiggle your butt faster, you're not Blending". "I'm trying dear, but the hoop's too small and it's chafing my rear-end!" "The hoop's not too small; your butt's too big." "Can't you get-into the rhythm, people are looking?" "What are you doing?" "You can't do that!" "Oh yes I can, I've got something to show-off - Michael Jackson did it, I watched his video!"

Six in the morning and time to leave. As I walked away from the stadium toward the metro station people were still dancing and partying in the streets adjacent to the Sambadromo. People would party twenty-four hours until the spectacular procession commenced at nine again for the second night in a row. Scalpers were already selling "Deluxe Concrete Seating" for the second night. "Sell you a Deluxe for $100 sir." "No thank you, I need to return to the hotel and catch-up on my sleep". "Nose bleeds for $75 sir." "Do you have any Granny's Deluxe Balcony Seating?" "No sir, but Uncle Jack has some Roof Seats at a good price." "Will I need a ladder?"

Humpty Dumpty

Barry Seymour Brett

Sitting on the Wall. Michael (La Gallina) playing Zamponya with his brother Julio and a friend

When I first arrived in Iquitos I did what most tourists and visitors would do. I took a casual stroll down the Boulevard on the banks of the Amazon River. Lined with bars and restaurants, the boulevard takes on a life of it's own in the warm jungle evenings. Swarms of rainforest people converge on the busy strip to watch the clowns performing in the pit. A wall stretches along the entire front. With only a limited amount of public seating, most people at sometime during their visit find themselves sitting on the wall. To be sure, there's ample seating inside and outside the restaurants and bars. However, since most jungle people have little or no money, bar and restaurant seating is off-limits.

During the 1960's the River Amazon took an abrupt turn, tearing-up the original wall built during the hey-days of the Rubber Boom. The rebuilt wall stands as testimony to the awesomely powerful river. Untamed by man, the River Amazon and its surrounding tributaries dominate the way of life and the customs and traditions of the Rainforest Peoples. City dwellers and rainforest kids sit on the wall without realizing its enormous significance. In Roman days a city without a wall was an open invitation to invading armies. The Chinese built the "Great Wall" to attract American tourists and to halt illegal trafficking in Noodles and Fortune Cookies. Walls are very symbolic. They signify security. Some people feel safe within their own four walls, especially from warrant-less searches! East Berliners were very "safe" inside their wall. They couldn't get-out for neither love nor money! But through time walls crumble. Just as the Boulevard Wall collapsed into the swirling Amazon, so in the end the Berlin Wall fell.

It was a warm weekend evening. There was a slight breeze blowing across the Amazon, the pre-cursor to a storm. Walking toward the wall I could see my friend Julio and his brother Michael who goes by the street name "La Gallina". Sitting on the wall, we were approached by police and politely asked to get-down. There had been a tragic accident the night before. A young man had fallen to his death. At various intervals along the wall there are steep steps reminiscent of those Georgetown steps featured so vividly in "The Exorcist". For several days following the tragedy, police patrolled the wall and politely asked people to get-down. Wall-sitters would briefly oblige, only to return moments later with more friends!

Sitting on the wall was a way of life, part of the Amazon tradition. Young men would sit waiting for their girls. Sometimes street musicians would sit on the wall and entertain the milling crowds. Families and friends would meet on the wall and wander over to the movie theatre. As news about the police action spread throughout the rainforest villages, large numbers of youths descended on the Amazon Boulevard the following weekend and proceeded to sit on the wall. More than fifty police and two large trucks arrived.

Sitting on the wall with Segundo, we watched as the cops hauled several teens over to the waiting trucks. Segundo spoke excellent English. "If we give-in to them we have no freedom left. What business is it of theirs? They are for criminals" "Barry, the boy who fell was stupid!" "What do you mean stupid?" "He was a jungle kid and he lost his balance. We climb trees all day long. It's his own fault. Why should we all suffer because of his stupidity?" "If we let the cops intimidate us here where will it stop?" "Today it's the wall, tomorrow it's the jungle." "They'll come and tell us we can't climb trees. My great grandfather was a rubber tree tapper and my uncle taps medicinal sap for the Belen Market." "If my uncle fell from a rubber tree would they ban climbers?" Would they cordon the trees off-limits - the entire rainforest maybe?" "But, aren't you afraid they might arrest you?" "They'll beat us and maybe torture us, but more of us will come. I have eight brothers." Alfonso, a cigarette vendor, called the police over and told them to leave everyone alone. "My safety depends on how much risk I want to take. What business is it of the police or the city? What good are all your laws if I enjoy jumping in-front of buses?"

Hundreds of youths defied the authorities and sat on the wall. Some kids stood precariously on the wall's edge while others did death-defying hand-stands along the entire length as police stood-bye and onlookers clapped. A man on stilts appeared and proceeded to taunt the police. Walking a stretch of the wall on stilts and then defying gravity as he stood balancing on one leg. Police marched several more kids across the street to the parked trucks. A crowd of young guys and some girls swarmed over toward the trucks. Jumping inside, they sat next to the arrestees and the cops! This entire time people in the crowd kept telling the cops to leave everyone alone and just go home! A couple of teens climbed-up the side of the adjacent hotel and proceeded to balance themselves on the window ledge. Every few minutes they would pretend to fall, calling-out "Ayudame" (Help me) I'm stupid! The following weekend there were no cops to be seen. The wall was free once again!

The Boulevard Wall along the banks of the Amazon River

Nighttime sitting on the Wall

"I thought-back to that tragic drowning on a San Diego beach. It was a young college girl. A student with a history of reckless behavior, she had been drinking beer with teenage friends. For many years the beach had been a popular hang-out for youths at weekends. Californian authorities shut the beach down. Signs were posted warning beachgoers not to trespass under penalty of fines or imprisonment! When the beach finally re-opened, police constantly harassed beachgoers asking for ID as they patrolled the area looking for anyone who might be drinking.

The beach was never the same again. Law-abiding beachgoers, feeling intimidated, abandoned the beach in search of other venues. Not the press, not the girl's parents and not even one member of the public suggested that maybe it was the student's own fault. Everyone pointed the finger at someone-else. The police were to blame for not enforcing underage drinking laws. The lifeguards were at fault for not patrolling that section of the beach. The city was to blame for not posting warning signs. Reckless teenage behavior did not exist. Everyone was living a lie! To add insult to injury, unlike the rainforest kids, not even one teenager challenged the police or the city to demand that the beach be re-opened, and that the girl be held at fault for her actions! A society born in freedom had lost its' will to fight.

"So he fell to his death did he? How dare he risk his life, and he wasn't even in the armed services. We'll put a stop to this reckless behavior. Climbing and balancing is henceforth outlawed. Falling to one's death is now a capital offence! The entire Rainforest is off-limits. Surround it with yellow trespassers' tape and post forty million signs. Rubber tree tappers and squirrels will need a permit, insurance, a hard-hat and a harness." "But sir, who gave you the authority to enforce these new laws?" "Sheep!"

Butterfly Alcatraz

Barry Seymour Brett

Butterfly Disguised as an Owl

Living in the city of Iquitos, smack in the center of the rainforest, I had often heard people talk about the Butterfly Farm. Most people went out to the farm to see the monkeys, the giant caged jaguar and to pet the giant anteater. As for me I had little real interest in viewing wild animals. Attacked and bitten by a dog whilst a child, I don't like animals, especially dogs, and they don't like me. Cats, well you know.

They've got those claws! I had a pet goldfish once. I felt safe watching it swim around in a bowl and I loved those trips to San Diego Zoo with my son. I like to look at exotic animals in a cage from a distance or on a plate with fries and coleslaw. It should come as no surprise, therefore, that when given an opportunity to visit the Butterfly Farm, I jumped at the chance. Peaceful, picturesque and non-threatening, butterflies were my kind of wildlife. Butterflies are elusive creatures. I had tried photographing them in flight using Kodachrome film and a 35mm camera. Just when I thought I had them in my viewfinder they would change direction and fly away! Setting the focus and aperture, while the elusive creatures slip away is now a thing of the past. I've gone digital! Now it's instant pictures in automatic focus. Ten megapixels has changed my life.

The butterfly farm was the creation of Gudrun, a devoted naturalist, dedicated to preserving rainforest wildlife. Gudrun and her Peruvian helpers had spent many hours day after day studying the life cycles and mating habits of the butterfly kingdom. The helpers spoke only Spanish. Gudrun was multi-lingual, speaking Butterfly, Caterpillar, German and English. Her command of Butterfly was second to none. It was rumored that she was raised as a child by a giant Amazonian moth. Terrified of cobwebs and cans of insect spray, Gudrun nevertheless overcame her phobias and now devotes her entire life to the preservation of butterflies. Whenever she had a spare moment, Gudrun would translate Butterfly into excellent English. Unfortunately because of her upbringing there was nothing fair or balanced about her commentary. It was always heavily biased in favor of butterflies and moths. In Gudrun's topsy-turvy world, butterfly nets would be outlawed and using formaldehyde to pin and fix them for display on a board would almost certainly be a capital offence!

Entering through a small gate we found ourselves in an enclosed area draped with netting on all sides. There were many more visitors and helpers than butterflies! Assistants would crawl on their hands and knees searching for rare butterfly species and their chrysalis's, only to be bitterly disappointed. There was precious little to photograph. A handful of imprisoned butterflies could be seen flying around in circles in a vain attempt to escape. There were several spectacular looking blue ones and a few owl butterflies. Disguised as owls they were obviously planning an early morning getaway. I couldn't help but wonder what had happened to all the butterflies. I've seen more moths in my closet than butterflies at the butterfly farm! But then maybe, just maybe, they were smarter than I thought. Their large wings caught-up in the netting, and having ran-out of owl-paint, they had come-up with an alternate escape route. Turning-into caterpillars they had obviously tunneled their way out of this "Butterfly Alcatraz".

Tunneling to freedom they would nevertheless be at the mercy of predators and butterfly nets. Free from the prying eyes of Commandant Gudrun and her goose-stepping assistants, they would eventually morph into beautiful butterflies once again and glide through the air, savoring the sweet aroma of freedom and liberty. As they flew away, no doubt they would wonder why they had tolerated Big Mother Gudrun for almost all of their pitifully short butterfly lives. They had been promised security inside the net. Their every whim and fancy would be catered for. They were guaranteed absolute safety from predators, free health care from Mother Gudrun and her ilk. With a guaranteed food program of free nectar and honey no butterfly would ever go hungry and "No Butterfly Left Behind". They had been tricked with smoke and mirrors. Lied to by Big Mother. Promised a world free of butterfly nets and insect repellant they had found themselves living beneath the biggest net of all with no chance of escape. All their cherished freedoms gone, sadly those beautiful colorful butterflies yearned for the day they would turn into ugly caterpillars and escape.

It was time to leave "Butterfly Alcatraz" and say goodbye to Big Mother. As I walked back down the narrow path toward the pueblo of Padre Cocha, I noticed a pair of beautiful butterflies gliding past on the warm Amazon breeze. I wondered to myself. Were they escapees who were once imprisoned within the netted fortress, or were they born free? Would they ever trade their freedom and liberty for Big Mother and the security of the safety net? As I reflected on their plight, I couldn't help wondering about us Californians. Would we trade-away all our freedoms for a safety net? Or have we already done so? Butterflies, those tiny insects, can teach us a lot about ourselves. The extremes of beauty and ugliness, and the conflict between safety, security and freedom and liberty.

Feliz Navidad

Barry Seymour Brett

Christmas Eve sing-song with Michael, Julio and some of his brothers, in their stilt-house above the River Amazon.

It was approaching midnight Christmas Eve. Jumping into a motokaro, I headed over toward the Belen Market and to "Las Escaleras" (The Steps) that led down to the stilt houses. My good friends the Sifuentes Family were expecting me. With eleven children and just a trickle of income from one of the boys, the family was always on the verge of starvation. Christmas dinner in the rainforest cities and villages is celebrated at midnight Christmas Eve. The Sifuentes are one of two families I support every Christmas. A couple of days earlier I had gone into the Belen market with the older kids and we had bought everything necessary for a good Christmas dinner. Paneton, Italian cake filled with fruit. Four "Live" turkeys, bananas, rice, sugar, flour, bread and cooking oil. They would not go hungry tonight.

The "Escaleras" leading down toward the Amazon River and the Stilt Houses. At the base of the steps was a different world.

Arriving at "Las Escaleras", Michael (La Gallina) and his older brother Julio were waiting at the top with two of their younger brothers. The long steep steps led down toward the stilt houses on the banks of the river Amazon. I had been down those steps many times. To help with medical emergencies in the middle of the night, to support their soccer team and just for the casual visit. Tourists and visitors seldom if ever descended the steps. Foreboding and sinister, they were not for the feint of heart, especially at night. At the base of the steps was a different world. Extreme poverty was the norm. To those that dwelt beneath the steps, Christmas would come and go, but nothing would change. There would be no celebration, no Christmas dinner, probably no food at all! A few weeks from now the river would rise forty feet and the only access would be by canoe.

The boys escorted me to their stilt house. Not that I didn't know how to find it! I'd been there many times in the past. But today was special. After Christmas dinner I would be taking them to "The International". They were not going to let me get away!

As I climbed-up the ladder into the stilt-house, I was greeted by mom and dad. It was a rare event. Unfortunately dad goes missing from the home for much of the year. All eleven children were present together with a couple of aunts who were helping with the cooking. Neighborhood youths, friends of the Sifuentes and Oscar Mala Suerte's mother dropped bye. No-one, absolutely no-one entered without first asking permission and shaking hands with the father. Maybe he was absent for much of the time, but when dad was home, respect for authority prevailed.

Sitting down on one of two long wooden benches I gazed at the assortment of food spread out across the table. Like magicians, and with very little to work with, the aunts had conjured-up a first class Christmas dinner. This, I thought, is how it must have been with the early American settlers. It's amazing what good women can do with so little. First it was a prayer to the good Lord, followed by a brief speech by dad. Thanking me, he emphasized to the family the importance of helping those less fortunate than themselves. Everyone clapped and then the feasting started.

After "Cena", Christmas Dinner, Julio and Michael entertained us all with Zampona and Guitar. Playing Feliz Navidad (the Christmas Song) and traditional songs about the rainforest and the river, the whole family joined-in. I took some Christmas pictures and video-clips with my camera and then the older boys left with me to the Christmas dance at the "International". Families and groups of youths stood at the bottom of the "Escaleras" staring enviously at us as we climbed upward. Arms around each other's shoulders, some of them waved-up at us and shouted "Feliz Navidad."

The "International" was the Ritz Carlton of the rainforest. A not very impressive three story structure, it stood directly facing the main Plaza. It was the preferred venue for the few wealthy Peruvians who could afford to rent it for a wedding fiesta or family birthday. The ballroom was on the upper level. Hundreds of kids milled about in front of the gates. Youths with tickets had saved-up all year for this annual event. Just to be able to say "I danced at the International", gave them status amongst their rainforest friends and neighbors.

Pier, Michael (La Gallina) and Jaime in the Plaza, waiting to enter the "International."

Entrance to the Stilt House of the Sifuentes Family below the steps

As I looked-down from the balcony toward the street below I could see a multitude of youths standing in the Plaza de Armas, looking enviously toward the "International". Few, if any, could afford the entry price. For them, Christmas Eve meant standing or dancing in the Plaza to the music blasting down from the balcony. As I stood on the ballroom balcony to cool-off from the heat of the interior, a young man approached and hugged me. It was Jay. I had taken him to the stadium for a soccer match back in July. We had ridden in the "Grand Caravana" with other friends. But why was he taking his shoes-off? Calling to a friend below the balcony, Jay threw down his shoes. The youth caught them and proceeded to put them-on. It was Oliver, Jay's best friend. A boxing champion at the college. "Barry, Oliver's got no shoes. The doorman won't let him in without shoes." "But Jay, doesn't he wear shoes when he boxes?" "No Barry, they box shoeless. They borrow shoes for tournaments!"

Returning to the fray, I bumped into Daniel, Alex the Zamponya player, and other kids I had come to know during the past year or two. Everyone was dancing wildly. Walking over to the bar with Oliver the boxer and Victor (the Midnight Planter) I noticed two girls waving frantically at me as they danced with their friends. It was Giselle and Rosa, the youths from the treetop party. But where was her boyfriend Elvis? The boy who was in love with Wendy the tree. "Barry, Elvis couldn't make it. He's got no shoes".

Surrounding the bar was a throng of kids, pushing and shoving, trying to attract the barman's attention. Few kids could afford to buy more than the standard "Three for ten" (Three bottles for ten Soles -$3). In this bar however it was "Three for twelve". Someone hugged me from behind as Victor the Midnight Planter humped the case of beer onto his shoulder. Hugging me like I was a long-lost brother (or someone who had just bought a case of beer), it was Oscar – Mala Suerte. Oh boy, I thought. Time to return to the bar and buy a second case!

Placing the case on the dance floor, Julio, Michael (La Gallina), Victor and now Oscar danced around it. We were soon joined by Oscar's brother, Giselle and Rosa. It was a wild dance. Reggae ton, a cross between Jamaican Reggae and Rap was blasting across the ballroom dance floor as young bodies pressed-up against me. Jay and some of the young guys showed-off their rapper hand-signs as they danced frantically to the music. For a moment I thought they were directing traffic on the Hollywood Freeway! This was not the Discotheque at Grandma's Outhouse in Barrio Florido! No washboard and jungle drums at this party. Several disco-balls swirled, illuminating the floor and walls with a multitude of colorful designs as powerful strobe lights flashed, highlighting the dancers as their bodies pulsated to the music.

Suddenly the music changed. The DJ screamed-out "La Anaconda". Youths rushed to form several long snaking columns. Victor the midnight planter and Giselle grabbed me as we all joined-in. Several snake formations wound their way across the dance floor as dancers motioned in a sexually suggestive manner. Oliver introduced me to his college girlfriend, Rosalina. A student for three years, she dropped-out when her parents couldn't pay. Rosalina, together with her neighborhood friend, Carina, joined the "Anaconda" as we all snaked our way around the dance floor.

Girls were attracted toward my bald head. A rare sight in the rainforest, young ladies would stroke and even lick my head! Suddenly the snake humped-up into the air like a giant caterpillar. Lifting my body clear off the ground, young guys supported me from behind as young ladies embraced me, twisting and frantically vibrating their bodies in rhythm to the music. It brought back memories of those belly dancers in Istanbul. My heart was pumping as I rode the serpent to the crest of the hump and started to descend. Six Flags Magic Mountain had nothing comparable to this! Everyone's dream, the ultimate sexual rollercoaster!

It was hot inside and just as I was about to walk over to the outside balcony to cool-off, the DJ announced the "Pandilla". An erotic mountain dance originating in Bolivia, the Pandilla is played at the Humisha Dance on Water Carnival Day. Youths broke-off from the Anaconda. Forming circles around beer bottles they danced the "Pandilla". The intense music drove everyone into a frenzy of excitement. Nothing like it exists anywhere else in the world.

It was gone five in the morning on Christmas Day and the fiesta at the International was winding-down. Moto taxi's out-front wanted double the normal fare, and you could be sure they would get it. Many of the revelers, almost all of them without money, would walk two or three hours to return to their village homes. They would arrive home on Christmas morning. For most there would be no "stocking", gift-wrapped presents nor mountains of food and cake. They would visit a neighbor or friend, wish them a Merry Christmas and return the shoes they had borrowed to dance at the "International".

FANTASY TRAP

Barry Seymour Brett

There it was across the street from the "Starbucks". Standing before me in all its' elegance. Bidding me, tempting me, compelling me. The glittering neon lights illuminated the gigantic parking lot in front of the "stop sign." Everyone would stop and shop. This was the "Twenty-Four Hour Walmart."

As I entered the store a voice spoke to me from within. "Welcome to Sam's Club". "Sam's Club, but I thought this was a Walmart". "You mean Uncle Sam?" - "but isn't he- "No, No Barry" "Uncle Sam's no more." "Back in the day, yes -but those days are long gone now". This is a "NEW WORLD UNCLE." "Uncle Sam is with **us** now." "We are one with him". "We are he, and he is us, and we are all together, koo koo ka choo, see how they buy, I am the Walmart, I am the Walmart, we are Sam's Man -koo koo ka choo. (Apologies to the Beatles).

"Feel the force within you Barry" "I am your Walmart; you know it to be true". "Yes, yes, I know" "It's useless trying to resist. I must shop and shop again." "Shop 'till I drop, shop 'till I drop." "Barry, it is your Destiny". "But Walmart, I want to return to the rainforest and the jungle, to the simple life." "Can't I switch the tractor beam off?" "No Barry, its way too late for that." "Walmart rules the Empire now, turn to the Mart-Side."

Suddenly I felt compelled to push the shopping cart. You know the one I mean. The cart with that twisted wheel that always steers into the nearest discount aisle. The cart that comes to a screaming halt just before you reach the car. Compelling you to return to your "Destiny". Then just when you think you've got away, there he is standing at the exit in full uniform. The Walmart Guard!

"Your discharge papers and exit visa sir? Oh, sorry sir, slip of the tongue. I meant your receipts." "But they're missing I can't find them." "Sir, take it-up with the manager in the morning." "But it's only 9pm!" "No problem Chip, it is Chip isn't it? This is a 24 hour Walmart, you can shop all night." "My name's Barry, not Chip. Oh, so that's it, I've been embedded!" "It's only temporary sir, we de-activate it once you've spent all your money and given us your soul." "My soul!" "Yes sir, this is the Mart-Side!" If only I could return to the rainforest, I thought. To the Amazon, the headhunters and witchdoctors, anacondas, mosquitoes and piranhas. Malaria, Typhoid, Yellow Fever. Anything would be better than the constant torment of a shopping aisle.

"But I'm meeting my son over at Starbucks. I have to leave now, I'm a customer". "Oh yes?" "We've heard that one before." "A customer?" "With a shopping-cart half-empty!" "Exactly what kind of customer are you?" "Where are you from?" "Give me your Driver's License, your PIN numbers and your DNA." "Maybe you were a customer when you came in but now you're a suspect." "A suspect?" "Yes sir, a suspect. Your cart's not full. You're under surveillance!"

Trapped at the exit I turned my cart around and headed back in. Wanting to call my son and without a cell phone, I would need a calling card. "We have the standard card for $20 or for $50 I could sell you our Premium Green. Guaranteed undetectable by Border Patrol, it comes with a bonus Social Security Card and a complete set of Driver's Licenses for all fifty States and the District of Columbia." "Oh, a phone card" "Sorry sir, we don't sell calling cards any more there's no money in it.' "By the way, do you sell fake Walmart Receipts; I need to get-out of here". "Afraid not sir, they're like gold". "Why don't you go talk to Carlos over at "Produce". "He crossed the Arizona border last night!"

Pushing my cart over to "Produce" I noticed a guy painting red tomatoes red. "Are you Carlos?" "What's with the brush and can of paint?" "It's FDA 40-RED, I'm painting-over the blemishes on the tomatoes." "Is it lead-based?" "No sir, it's just government approved food-coloring mixed with varnish to give them a shine." "Can you help me? I need to leave." "I'm supposed to meet my son over at Starbuck's." "Sir, getting into the US without documents, that's easy." "Leaving Walmart's without receipts, next to impossible" "They want proof that you've spent your money - all of it!"

"Why don't you apply for a job, then you could leave through the employee's entrance in the back?" "Are they hiring? "Yes, I crossed the border last night and they hired me right away." "But I don't look very Hispanic." "Maybe if you painted yourself with FDA 23-BROWN". "They sell baggy pants and Mexican Bandanas made in China on aisle 36. If they don't hire you we might have to smuggle you out!"

"Good luck with your escape" Carlos shouted, as I sped over the border from Walmart's to Starbuck's in the trunk of a car. "If they catch you and send you back I have friends who can dig a tunnel!"

Save the Eco-Coffee

Barry Seymour Brett

Sitting in a comfortable armchair I noticed the Rainforest paintings on the wall. Outlines of indigenous peoples, jungle fauna and banana plantations. Illustrations of happy, smiling people carrying baskets of coffee beans on their shoulder. I felt like I was already back in the Amazon Jungle. In the far-corner someone was handing-out "Adopt-a-Thon" leaflets. "For only five dollars a month you too can adopt a Rainforest Orphan" "Write them letters and share photos." That's funny, I don't recall seeing anyone from Starbucks, or anyone else for that matter, handing-out five dollar bills to Rainforest kids! All they ever did was buy-up the best quality coffee beans in Brazil and Columbia, leaving the low grade beans for the "Wonderful Indigenous People". No wonder immigrants swarm into the U.S. from Brazil and Columbia. They can't find a good cup of coffee down there!

"Hi honey, lets go down to Starbucks and adopt a Rainforest Child." "It's the in-thing amongst the upwardly mobile." "We won't be the least bit inconvenienced; she'll live such a long, long way away." "It's only five dollars a month; we can share photos and pretend it's our child." (The child we'll never have because we're so greedy and selfish). "But honey, can't we have one of our own?" "No way!" "Get a life woman, we need to make the house-payments, trade-in the car for an SUV and drink Frappaccinos and Cranberry Iced Mochas. "Maybe in a year or two." "But I'm almost over the hill, it's getting too late."

"Where's your head at gal, haven't you ever heard of egg transplants?" "We could check the yellow pages. "Rent-a-Womb" has a special offer right-now. Twins - two for the price of one! Third world women love to do things like that!"

Then there's that corporate responsibility leaflet. You know the one I mean, they've all got them now. Coffee growers are praised for conserving water usage when there's enough freshwater in the Great Lakes alone to supply the entire planet. That doesn't include the River Amazon, the largest body of freshwater in the world! I couldn't help but reflect on our disastrous attempts at imposing our warped western values and lop-sided ideas about fairness upon the indigenous peoples.

Rainforest people don't believe in fairness. It's seen as a form of socialism, a way to level the playing field to the lowest common denominator. Naive westerners who promote fairness are perceived as weak and become easy prey to a people who believe in taking advantage of any situation that comes along. Fair wages and fair labor practices! Why? Their very environment teaches them that strong animals kill weaker ones. Malaria and yellow fever are equal opportunity killers. There's nothing fair about being attacked by piranhas, anacondas or bolts of lightning. Fairness can't exist amongst the rainforest. It's a man-made concept that can only exist when imposed upon the people by government authorities who have no intention of practicing it themselves. The jungle knows what we once knew but have long since forgotten. Fairness is fantasy. An alien concept with no validity.

"Hi, how can I help you?" "Mr. Brett, did you purchase a lottery ticket at Jack's Grocery Store?" "Why, yes" "Congratulations on winning the California State Lottery, you've won twelve million dollars!" "Oh gosh, this is awesome news. I can re-connect the electricity and go get grandma's gold necklace out of the pawn shop". "Yes sir, here's your check". "But where's the twelve million, this check's for only one dollar". "Yes sir, there's nothing fair about the California Lottery; it relies on winners and losers. That's why we've split the winnings up with the losers so they can feel good about themselves." "But I bought a two dollar sweep, where's the other dollar?" "Uncle Sam took it - it's only fair that he should have half!" As I glanced at the fancy cookies and German chocolate cake, I asked myself just how fair and balanced Californians really are. If I'm smart and my neighbor's dumb, should I dumb myself down just to be fair to him? If my house collapses in an earthquake, is my neighbor obligated to give me half of his? Whilst preaching fairness Californians practice something else!

The Starbucks store was packed solid with customers spending their petro-dollars, drinking from environmentally friendly re-cycled coffee cups. Ordering a "Double Skinny Vanilla Latte", I noticed the young man's fashion statement. A blue light flashed in his ear. "The Blue Tooth!" "Swipe the card sir - yes I do love you, I think of you every night" "Wait a minute, I don't even know you". "Not you sir, I'm talking to my girl on Bluetooth." "Well, turn it off, I'm a customer." "I can't hang-up or she'll multitask with someone else." "Well, whatever happened to love and romance?" "Oh, that's old school, if she won't multitask I'll drop her" "Multitask, but with how many?'" Two, three, sometimes four." "Four!" Are you on Viagra?" "No sir, you don't get it, we just talk trash over the Bluetooth."

As I waited for my son I looked at the customers manipulating their electronic devices. Blackberries, I-Phones, I-Pods, Cell-Phones, Apple-Macs and Laptops. The odd person engaged in conversation over his Bluetooth. A couple of love-birds entered and sat down in front of me. Talking to each other via their Bluetooth's, there was no body language, no intimacy and probably no love! Everybody seemed to be "linked", but nobody seemed to be "alive." Could this really be the world we've created for ourselves? A world of Iced Mochas and electronic data links.

"Hola, que tal?" (Hello, how's things?) We missed you." "Just got-back from California, Roberto, I'd like an Iced Frapaccinno and a slice of German Chocolate Cake." "Sorry sir, we've got Powdered Nescafe or Low-Grade Brazilian Bean coffee." "Do you have Wi-Fi, I need to hook-up?" "No, she's busy in the back with another customer, maybe later in the day!" "But my sister's here sir." "Yes, I could exchange data with your sister. Just to be fair, I should multitask with them both later-on! "Sir, how is it up there in California? I hear it's a paradise." "Yes it is. Californians are on a huge dopamine rush. They fuel-up on

Red Bull energy drinks and swig-down triple caffeine shots at the nearest Starbucks. Everyone's multitasking, Googleing, Twittering, Face Booking, My Spacing, Data-mining, Blue-toothing and Blackberrying." "But sir, do they still make love and have children?" "It's a new world up North my friend, there's no time left to do much of anything else." "Tell me about the Bluetooth sir, does it come with dental floss? When you multitask with my sister and, (just to be fair) - with her friend, will you be using the Blue Tooth?" "No, we'll be using Viagra the Purple Pill!"

Save the Eco-Coffee
The person handing-out Adopt-a-Thon leaflets was not an employee of Starbucks' Coffee! Starbucks does help many small impoverished communities in Africa and South America.

The Remedy

Barry Seymour Brett

There was a knock at my door. Antonio had received an urgent message. His uncle was dying. He needed money to go visit the village, two days downriver. "But Antonio, the last time I lent you money for an emergency, friends saw you drinking in the Red Moon Hooker Bar; the very same night!" "Barry, this is different, it's my uncle. He's dying". "OK Antonio, let's go visit him together". It was a chance to return to Requena, a small river port on the banks of the river Maranon. I had fond memories of the town, having visited it with some good friends several years before.

Entering the house I noticed a group of relatives standing around the bed. Antonio's aunt told us that the doctor had just left. They had been told to expect the worse, but nevertheless they were to continue with the treatments. The doctor had strung leeches around the man's throat to suck-out the venom! A woman from next-door massaged his withering joints with lizard ointment as an elderly man shoved a bamboo tube down the throat and proceeded to drip a concoction into it. Antonio's uncle heaved and struggled to remove the bamboo tube. But it was probably too late. Inseminated with the concoction it would be only a matter of time before the alien creature would burst-out of his stomach, scurry along the floor with its tentacles, and spray vitriolic acid all over the hut and everyone inside.

Antonio cried. He had never seen his uncle this sick before. A man stood in the shadows shaking a painted rain-stick (bamboo stick containing jungle seeds). Antonio told me the man was counting-down the remaining hours of life. News spread fast throughout the town that an American had come to offer assistance. Villagers arrived bringing new remedies in the hope of making an extra buck or two. A local shaman dropped-by. For a few dollars he could cleanse the man's soul and prepare him for death! What was wrong with trying to keep him alive I thought? Visiting a local pharmacy I bought some shots, antibiotics and vitamin pills.

On returning we were greeted by an elderly woman who claimed she had important information regarding Antonio's uncle. His wife had a secret lover. Later that evening two young boys came-by. Claiming to have "hot news" they wanted two bottles of inka-cola and a loaf of bread. As we returned from the corner store carrying the soda and bread the boys described how Antonio's aunt was secretly seeing their neighbor. There was a gaping hole in the side of the hut and the two of them had been seen together late at night, naked, and they weren't just holding hands. Every twist and turn was described in excruciating detail. It was the best the boys had seen and those peeping toms had seen a lot! Their neighbors' hut was not the only hut in town with a gaping hole it seemed. "Nothing was left to the imagination." Just what kind of secret lover was he I wondered, when the whole town seemed to know about it. Maybe he was an exhibitionist!

The following morning the plot thickened. A man who lived across from the local cemetery described in vivid detail how her secret lover had been seen draining water from the graveyard and collecting it in a bottle! Two workers at the local mortuary arrived. They had heard that a rich American was paying money for information! Not wanting to tell tells, at least not without a propina (tip, bribe), they told us how a man approached them and purchased a bottle of water after it had been used to bathe the dead! The same man had been seen late at night, sprinkling the "death water" on the roof of Antonio's uncle's hut.

Not wanting to be out-maneuvered, the local shaman re-appeared later in the day and announced that with the new information at hand, the man could be saved. All what was needed was to place rows of coins of the realm across the victim's chest. Everyone in the neighborhood was required to place a coin on the man's chest. Failure to do so would come with "grave" consequences. In the meantime, under pressure from relatives and neighbors, the aunt confessed and broke down in tears. Yes, she had sprinkled graveyard juice all-over her husband while he slept!

Antonio was very upset. I forced some more antibiotics and vitamins down his uncle's throat, (without the bamboo tube), while neighbors arrived and placed coins on his chest. We took a walk down to the dockyard market and had something to eat. Upon returning to the hut we were surprised to see Antonio's uncle sitting-up in bed talking. But where were all the coins of the realm? Where was the shaman? "Oh he left town with the coins, his works done!" "But I thought he was the local shaman?" "No, he's a travelling shaman. They roam from town to town looking to help the sick and dyeing". "Yes, Antonio. Living-off the coins of the realm!"

On the third day the vitamins kicked-in and Antonio's uncle was on the way to a full recovery. The boat for Iquitos left in the afternoon. As we sailed along the River Maranon I thought about people back home. When I return to California I'd like to conduct a "sprinkling". Starting with the Department of Motor Vehicles and ending up at the Governor's Mansion. Unfortunately liquids and bottles are no-longer permitted in overhead bags!

Barrio Barry

Barry Seymour Brett

It was gone midnight and things were winding-down on the Amazon Boulevard. I jumped into a moto-taxi and headed home. As the taxi turned the corner into my street I could hear loud music and see a large group of youths and a smattering of adults. They were dancing and drinking in front of the corner house as loud music blasted-out across the street from two speakers perched on the window ledge. It was a Barrio Fiesta. A street birthday party for Jonathon's nineteenth. There would be no cake and no tears at this birthday party. This was the Barrio and everyone and everything was up-for-grabs. And at this party everyone and "everything" would be grabbed!

"Welcome to the Barrio Barry". "Oh, is that Miguel over there? Come-on guys, help me lift him up!" "Oh, just leave him there Barry, he'll only fall-down again" "But where's Jonathon?" "Oh don't worry about Jonathon right now; he's busy throwing-up in the backyard!" "Who are the girls?" "Linda and Rosa, Jonathon's sisters and the tall one is Ema." "Who are they, the girls throwing Carlos into the bushes?" "They are Barrio girls from the other end of the street. Maybe they're strong but they're sweet and we "all love them".

This was not Los Angeles or the Valley. This was not the typical Mexican Immigrant Barrio. These youths didn't need to hide behind guns and knives, gang colors and slogans to cover-up their weaknesses. Even the girls were big and strong. These young men, all muscled-up, would carry buckets of water to their house in the day, and then climb trees (without shoes or ladder) tapping for rubber and medicinal herbs. These barrio boys and girls, thought nothing of walking six or seven miles to school or work each day, up to their ankles in mud; many of them bare-footed. In a world without cement mixers, running water, cranes and pick-up trucks their very survival depended on muscular strength. Recreation for many of them meant playing soccer, barefooted on a concrete street or in a swampy clearing swarming with insects and crawling with snakes!

"Barry, you have to join-in, you can't just sit there." "But I only wanted to buy you guys some booze and say hi to Jonathon and his girl" "You can't just leave, we want you to stay, you're one of us." "But Jose, it's one-thirty in the morning and I need to go sleep a while". "This is the Barrio; you live on our street, we are the Barrio and so are you." Suddenly several guys jumped on me as I sat on the bench. Pulling me-up amongst the throng they danced, humped and poked around my body as girls joined-in. Were they all just super-horny or was this my initiation into the Barrio I wondered? Maybe this is what they do when they want someone to buy more beer! Several guys lifted me-up onto their shoulders and paraded me amongst the group before carrying me down the street to the liquor store. Buying two bottles of cheap Tarapoto wine, we returned to the fiesta. Ema stood behind the open window where she mixed the wine with other ingredients to concoct the "trago especial". This potent mixture was always referred to as "Sex in the Jungle".

As I returned to the throng, guys poured-out the trago as girls dragged me back amongst the revelers. Passers-bye would stand and watch and cheer-us-on. Moto-taxi's driving past would honk their horns. They would watch but not join-in. This was a Barrio Fiesta and they knew it was off-limits to strangers. Everyone was dancing with everyone. Youths would gang-up on someone and suddenly pounce; just like the jungle animals they had seen so many times before. Slamming him against a tree trunk, the wooden bench or the lamp post they would dance around him with the girls. Spread-eagled they would pull-down his pants! Thirty years in California and I'd never seen a private party like this before! Yet this was no "private party". This was a street party in full public view! A Police cruiser (Serenazco) passed-bye. Honking their horn and cheering us on, they parked across the street and watched for two or three minutes before leaving. Young or old; made no difference. There were several adults, although most the partiers were in their late teens or early twenties. Just when it seemed to be dying down the music changed and I was swept-up amongst their midst once again. Guys paraded me spread-eagled across the street as girls pulled down my pants and someone ran-off with my baseball cap! All this time loud music blasted-out from the window ledge speakers as everyone cheered.

"Barry, you're the only blanco (white) in our Barrio, they wanted to see if "everything" was bien blanco (very white!)." "But Francisco, they weren't just looking!" "Well, that's because the girls and the guys like to know who is the "Manchingar". "The Manchingar?" "Its' rainforest myth going way-back to the ancient Incas" "We share our bodies. We're in touch with our bodies and we touch and caress each other. It's part of who we are." "The Manchingar; its street slang for the biggest in the Barrio! It has it's origins with the African slaves brought to Brazil to work in the coffee plantations." "Well, am I the new Manchingar?" "No Barry, Miguel is still Manchingar." "Miguel! But he's snoring on the ground next to his beer." "Barry, I hear they sell Manchingar Pills in California. Could you bring me some back? Rainforest girls like Manchingars."

Waking-up late the following morning, I felt refreshed and contented. Finally I had found my niche, thousands of miles from home. A small street in an isolated jungle city had taken me into their midst and welcomed me into their exclusive club. Strangers and outsiders beware; I've mind-melded and "body-melded" with the Barrio. You need to keep your distance from me now. I thought-back to the words of Jose at the Barrio Fiesta. "This is the Barrio; you live on our street, we are the Barrio and so are you" Suddenly I realized why Mom had named me Barry. Mom must have known all along that I would end-up here in the Barrio. I belong in the Barrio with the Manchingars. I am part of the Barrio. I am Barrio Barry! What a shame; Mom forgot to mix Manchingar pills with my bowl of cereal!

Rendezvous With Pink & Grey

Barry Seymour Brett

I felt the boat was a little too small. I like the big ones. You know, the ocean going liners with swimming pools, casinos, movie theatres and life-boats. Yes, life-boats. Especially the life-boats. I can't swim! I feel safe in a big ship (did someone mention Titanic?). There's something intimidating about a small boat. The water always seems too close to the top! Oops, now it's splashing-over. Time to pray! The current was strong and the boat was struggling to maintain speed as we went further downriver. Someone mentioned the piranhas. Locals tell you not to fear piranhas. They won't attack. Sorry guys, I just don't believe it. Their teeth remind me of a baby shark or that dog that bit me when I was a child. The Captain and crew handled the navigation superbly and soon we were heading for our rendezvous with pink and grey dolphins. "Barry, no-one, absolutely no-one eats dolphin meat". "Why's that Daniel? I imagine it would taste real good." "The local people consider it bad-luck." How strange I thought; rainforest people eat fruit-eating rats, all kinds of snakes, even guinea pigs and monkeys, but somehow dolphins are off-limits and bad luck. After all it wasn't so-long ago that they were eating each other and shrinking their neighbors' heads! Luck can't get much worse than that!

Some biologists claim that pink dolphins are super intelligent. It's even been said that they communicate with dolphins on distant planets! Supposedly pink dolphins sing and even talk to each other. I wonder if female pinks keep talking and never shut-up! Could be that they have underwater marriage ceremonies amongst the corals. Scientists claim that dolphins are "just like humans" and mate for life staying with the same partner!!!! I guess there are no underwater dolphin divorce courts but there sure are a bunch of human ones on the surface!

Before leaving Iquitos I was warned not to get my hopes-up. There would probably be plenty of opportunities to see and photograph the Greys, but the Pinks were a different breed entirely. For many visitors and naturalists, a glimpse (and that's probably all they'll get) of a pink dolphin would be the highlight of their trip to the Amazon. Pinks are the stars and the Greys are nothing more than a pleasant background of supporting actors. Why, I wondered, are the Pinks supreme whilst the Greys languish in obscurity? Is it simply that there are so few of them? Or could there be a pecking-order? Is it a case of "Pink Skin Rules?" Are the Grays protected by underwater affirmative action or are they still struggling for emancipation? Surely the Greys yearn for the day when they will achieve equality with the Pinks; their grey bald heads stroked and petted by doting tourists.

There were several opportunities to take photos of the grey dolphins. They would jump clear-out of the river and perform acrobats as passengers looked-on in amazement. Grey dolphins were not shy in front of humans and were capable of mesmerizing their admirers with a spectacular acrobatic show. But where were the elusive Pinks? It was late in the afternoon when someone sighted a pink dolphin in the distance. Once in a while, once in a long, long while, a dolphin would surface and reveal its pink bald head. Graceful and serene I felt an affinity with them. Just like me, they were embarrassed about their baldness. Sentenced to a lifetime of baldness these beautiful creatures yearned for a brush and a comb, a trip to the barber, and a bottle of shampoo. I could feel their pain. Is it no-wonder they didn't surface for very long? We had been told that it would possible to pet them, but on this trip they never came close enough. Some passengers claimed to have petted Pinks on a previous trip.

Our dolphin rendezvous accomplished we sailed further down the River Amazon toward the Giant Lilly Pads. Named after Queen Victoria these gigantic pads can grow ten feet wide or more. We pulled-into various small ports, coves and lagoons where we met local tribes. Most the passengers spoke no Spanish. When you can't speak the local tongue, sign language works. The Dollar Sign! Villagers displayed their handicrafts and performed traditional dances. There were necklaces made from various colored seeds and fruits. Crocodile and piranha teeth. Purses, wallets and hand-bags made from locally woven cloth, or from animal skins. Poison dart blow-guns, the perfect gift for mother-in-law. A large selection of wood and bone carvings and all kinds of menacing-looking voodoo dolls dressed in traditional clothes. There were key-rings with hand-carved dolphins and small mirrors surrounded by colorful shells and beads. I thought I saw a shrunken head, but it was just my reflection! I think I need plastic surgery.

Always impressive on a river trip are the jungle trees that line the shore. Such an amazing variety of trees and ferns not seen anywhere else on the planet. Every now and again young boys and girls would run-up to the shore's edge and wave as we sped-bye. The small boat with a limited number of passengers provided an intimacy sadly lacking on the larger vessels that ply the Amazon. We actually got to know each other. I quickly discovered who the strong swimmers were! Passengers exchanged emails and experiences on other trips. I might even go-out on another tour myself, after my plastic surgery and swimming lessons!

Welcome to IQUITOS

Barry Seymour Brett

I wasn't really heading for Iquitos. Like most tourists who visit Peru my primary target was Cuzco and the ancient Inca ruins of Machu Picchu. Iquitos, a giant trading post on the Amazon River was to be no-more than a stop-over while I rested and scoped-out a shipping line to take me downriver to Manaus. Then overland to Brazilia and Rio for Carnival. I thought a week or two in Iquitos would do the trick. A week turned into a month and the months turned into years! I found the City fascinating. What's more, passengers arriving up-river from Manaus had nothing nice to say about the boring trip! The food on board was "worse than hospital food!" and theft was rampant. Then there were those popular T-shirts sold in Rio. "I lost my heart in Rio - My camera, my wallet, my watch".

I arrived in drizzle on a Thursday. The City was dead. But by Friday night Iquitos morphed into a beautiful butterfly, vibrant and colorful. Hundreds of people from the surrounding villages descended on the Boulevard and Plaza de Armas for a night-on-the -town. Music blasted-out from bars and restaurants lining the banks of the Amazon while clowns and monkeys performed for the general public. There was a guinea pig surrounded by tiny numbered houses. Poor piggy was put inside a sack, swirled-around until dizzy and then dropped into the center. People placed bets as to which house he would run to! Seemed cruel to me. My son had a pet guinea pig once. We loved her. Even had a backyard funeral when she passed away. But a live, dizzy guinea pig in a sack, beets a dead one on a plate. I quickly realized the locals roast them on a spit!

There were wandering bands playing Zamponyas and drums. Traditional dancers wearing almost nothing danced around giant snakes. People wearing almost nothing flocked to the local discothèques and beer and wine flowed everywhere. Yes, Iquitos is a partying town at weekends. The people are so loving and caring. Warm and friendly, they take care of your every whim and fancy. Nothing is left to imagination, it's the real thing.

Saturday boasts a display of Capuera on the Boulevard. An unusual combination of African chants and karate. Young men and women perform the difficult and dangerous maneuvers with precision and skill. Originating amongst the Brazilian negro slaves it evolved over hundreds of years into it's present form.

I took a side-trip into Belen, the local market. All kinds of unusual and varied fruits and fish were on display. The strangest, ugliest fish in the world swim nearby. There was a whole street devoted to medicinal plants and ointments made from the Boa Constrictor, Crocodiles and fish. There was a stand where they mixed strange brightly-colored bubbling concoctions to cure every illness known to man. I felt like I was on another planet. I glanced behind looking for the Aliens playing flutes or someone brandishing a light saber.

Then there were the artisans displaying a multitude of artifacts. Necklaces made of crocodile teeth. Coconuts and strangely-shaped fruits carved into monkeys or weird-looking jungle dolls. I wanted to stick pins in them. I looked for one resembling my ex-wife or my congressman! There were a multitude of colored beads made from various jungle seeds and berries. Anaconda and crocodile skins and furs from lamas and tigers. Menacing painted piranhas, frozen and perched on a stand, ready to spring to life and attack the innocent by-stander. Oops, there goes another finger!

I grew-up in England. I enjoy soccer. I thought I'd seen it all. You know, those wild out-of-control soccer fans. Welcome to Max Austin Stadium, Iquitos, Peru. It seemed innocent enough. I noticed people brightly painted entering the stadium with drums, shields and even spears. Oh, great, we're getting entertainment at half-time. Foolish me.

Within minutes the ugly chants started-up, getting louder as each side vied for attention. Rioters, (I mean supporters) on both sides beat their shields with spears and howled menacing threats across the field. Screeching high-pitched hoots enveloped the surrounding stands as the drums of both sides beat-out their supporting chants. Police in riot gear surrounded the stands. It had more in common with ancient Rome than a modern soccer match. Only the lions and gladiators were missing. Suddenly these loving peaceful people were transformed into the wild beasts that surround their habitat. I turned to a friend. Surely these are not the same people who stroll the Boulevard at night? Oh no Barry. These are University students!

What an amazing place Iquitos is. Those floating houses on stilts! I guess they just didn't want to pay for a piece of land. They let the trash pile-up underneath, spreading infections and feeding the rats. I guess they didn't want to pay the trash collector either! Finally the river rises some forty feet, washing the trash downstream and everyone rides around in small boats. Maybe the stilts have more to do with the small stature of most Iquitenos. It makes them feel tall! Someone told me there were plans to build a golf course in town. Now wouldn't that be something. A golf course on stilts! The eighth wonder of the world!

Every type of jungle tour was on-offer. Young men wander up and down the boulevard and hang-out in front of hotels offering the most amazing boating and jungle adventures imaginable. Their motto is "take the money and run!". More reputable outfits operate out of the front of hotels or even have their own office suites on the Boulevard or on Prospero, the main drag. I soon realized who the fakes were. If they spoke good English I was in trouble. After all, they learnt English for a reason. Not to help me, but to take advantage of me! And do they put the screws in good. Only my divorce attorney did better - but he promised me!!!

The weather. Well at four degrees south of the equator, it was awesome. Not too humid, hot in the day but only warm at night. Nothing like those sweltering nights I remembered so well in humid Maryland and Virginia. A cooling breeze blows thru the Amazon River and the frequent rain cools things-off. After thirty years in Southern California, I found the city climate inviting and the evenings relaxing. Missing from the scene were, McDonald's, Burger King, Domino's Pizzas, Barnes and Nobles, Starbuck's Coffee House and Walmart. Missing, but not missed

Copyright July 2009

Celebrating the Rebellion Against the Crown

Barry Seymour Brett

Barry Brett celebrating the Rebellion against the Crown at the Amazon Golf Course on July 4th 2009

Well I was born and raised in England and went to school and college there. Worked my first few jobs there, but always inside I was American! While other children happily read Beano and Dandy Comics I was hooked on Mickey Mouse Weekly. Those Disney cartoons were everything to me. As I grew-up I slicked-back my hair, put on my blue jeans (American Levis) and slid into my Blue Suede Shoes. Yes I was in love with Elvis and American Rock and Roll. So it should come as no surprise that having traveled much of the world by age twenty two, I found myself finally in the U.S., sitting on the Florida sand at Coco beach together with some two million Americans watching the Apollo launch to the Moon. I never really left! I've lived in the U.S. more than forty years and now I find myself completely Americanized with only a slight trace of that perfect English accent I once had. I think of myself as American. My Son was born in California and my wife was Californian. So there I was at the Amazon Golf Course, Iquitos, Peru, celebrating the Rebellion against the Crown!

By the time we arrived it had been raining heavily. It's the Rainforest! Bill Curtis was upstairs in the clubhouse playing flute entertaining Bill grimes and other Americans who had dropped-by to celebrate the Rebellion. I wanted to ask Bill to play "Yankee Doodle Dandy" but then I realized I'd forgotten the words. I could have sung "God save the Queen". I still remember those words, but somehow it just didn't seem appropriate. Did it ever seem appropriate? Waltzing Matilda sounds even more bizarre. Who was Matilda anyway? I've got my own ideas on that one but I wouldn't want to offend my Aussie friends! But "God save the Queen". What was she doing that was so bad that she had to be saved!

Bill Curtis playing flute for the July 4th celebration at the Amazon Golf Course Clubhouse.

I settled for hot dogs and the "Star-Spangled Banner". The hot dogs (Brazilian Sausage) together with beans and potato salad were excellent, as was all the American cuisine. I chugged-down a couple of "Inca Colas" and the beer drinkers stuck to their favorites, Pilsen or Iquitena. It was quite a treat after so many months of fake American food in Arie's Burger and the other Boulevard restaurants. Surrounded by Red, White and Blue balloons, it felt like America even though we were thousands of miles away from home.

There was plenty of good music, dancing and golfing in the rain for those so inclined. Dancing is not permitted on the golf course unless totally drunk! Then there's an additional fee to remove all the empty six-packs or was it beer kegs?

Celebrating the Fourth at the Amazon Golf Course

It was a mixed bunch. There were other Brits celebrating the loss of the Colony; that kick-in-the-teeth, chop-off the hand that fed you (and TAXED YOU!). Or maybe it was just an excuse to chug-down some more beer. After all there are plenty of Americans who see the Fourth as nothing more than an excuse to party-down. As for me the Fourth represents much more than that.

Yes, THE FOURTH. Notice that Americans never describe it as the Fourth of July. To us it's THE FOURTH. It represents a sea-change in political thought. Those TRAITORS (Oh, I mean those HEROES) who risked a public hanging to give the world a new concept of governance. The notion that the rights of man are god-given and not the property of Kings and Queens, Emperors and Despots. Rights that are god-given and cannot be abridged or taken away without the express consent of the governed. I was celebrating the founding documents, the Constitution, Declaration and Bill of Rights. The world has never been the same since. There was a time once, when I was a child walking to school through the ruins and rubble of my totally destroyed hometown when the "Stars and Stripes" meant everything to everyone. Americans were heroes and welcomed everywhere as liberators. Oh gosh, the American flag, the "Stars and Stripes". Have I been color-blind all these years? Is it? Yes it is. RED, WHITE and BLUE. No, it can't be, but surely it is. Aren't those the same colors from the British flag, the "Union Jack"? No they wouldn't would they? I mean that's trans-Atlantic thievery. Steal the colors after kicking the Brits in the teeth. OH YES THEY WOULD!

JUNGLE FREEZE-FRAME FACTS

Lewis the street vendor came over my house for my birthday party and again at Christmas. He has not recovered from the tragic loss of his baby girl six months ago.

The fiesta in a treetop was one of many highlights of my life in Iquitos. My only regret is not having my camera with me. It was a spur of the moment thing.

There have been numerous incidents of tourists being bitten by monkeys. Not only at the Butterfly Farm but at other locations as well. Graciela Mapacocha, a fisherwoman of Santo Tomas, was attacked by a twenty-foot boa constrictor. The second such attack in less than a year. A tourist, groping for a golf ball, lost the tip of his finger to a giant piranha at the Amazon Golf Club recently.

With very few exceptions, almost all of the personalities described in my storylines currently live in Iquitos or the surrounding rainforest. Several of the young men have left, looking for work in Lima, over a thousand miles away. Most will return after a few months. Eventually "La Energia de la Selva" (The Energy of the Jungle) lures them back to their cultural roots.

Yes, some teachers were drunk at the school promotion. Escorting three prizewinning students to the airport, we waited in vain for their teacher. He arrived drunk; thirty minutes after the plane had left. The students' parents had only nice things to say about him. "It's ok, it was his birthday and he went out drinking with friends, what's wrong with that?" What's wrong with that is that I viewed the situation through the eyes of a Californian and they viewed it through the prism of the rainforest.

The Brazilian Pirate Boat was not called the "Lust" and the storyline is in fact a combination of two separate encounters with smugglers. More amazing things happened than I describe in the story. I just did not think readers would believe it all! I met Veronica the pirate at Port Henry again the following year, whilst waiting for a passage to Leticia, Columbia. It was meeting her the second time that triggered a desire to write the story

I've seen babies, other than Oscar's baby, in cardboard boxes several times in front of the Casa de Fierro.

Wilber the Tarot Card Man is a close neighbor. Beware, look-over your shoulder, he still carries-out investigations.

I've since been told that some of the guards at the Penal do have ammo! Would you want to take a chance? Cheverengue is out of jail now. I met him recently at a soccer match here in Iquitos. Hulk, whose real name is Manuel, currently works in construction here in the city. Robinson muerto (dead one) was released last month. Sadly his six year-old daughter has just died of a chest infection.

The ayahuasca session was much more grotesque than the watered-down version in my storyline. But it is a fact that most people who participate in the ayahuasca ceremonies come away feeling renewed and re-energized.

I've ridden several caravanas during the past year alone. They are fun and very exciting. They are so much fun that some supporters of the losing team will still join-in!

Many families rely on their young children to go out and work. Without the income that these small children provide, the whole family would suffer. There would be no money to pay for food, aspirin or simple medicines and something as common as a fever could and often does become fatal. Some taxi drivers are twelve years old or less. They drive responsibly and carefully. When children are allocated responsible tasks they mature faster and grow into well-rounded adults.

To order additional copies of this book please visit the website;
www.junglefreezeframe.com

www.ingramcontent.com/pod-product-compliance
Lightning Source LLC
Chambersburg PA
CBHW031208270326
41931CB00006B/459